In the Name of Emmett Till

ALSO BY ROBERT H. MAYER

When the Children Marched:
The Birmingham Civil Rights Movement

The Civil Rights Act of 1964

In the Name of Emmett Till

How the Children of the
Mississippi Freedom Struggle
Showed Us Tomorrow

ROBERT H. MAYER

FOREWORD BY LESLIE-BURL MCLEMORE

NEWSOUTH BOOKS
Montgomery

NewSouth Books
105 S. Court Street
Montgomery, AL 36104

LIBRARY OF CONGRESS CATALOGING-IN-PUBLICATION DATA
Names: Mayer, Robert H., 1950– , author.
Title: In the name of Emmett Till : how the children of the Mississippi freedom struggle
showed us tomorrow / Robert H. Mayer.
Description: Montgomery, AL : NewSouth Books, [2021] | Includes bibliographical
references and index. | Audience: Ages: 12–18 | Audience: Grades: 6–12.
Identifiers: LCCN 2021001808 (print) | LCCN 2021001809 (ebook) | ISBN
9781588384379 (hardback) | ISBN 9781588384454 (ebook)
Subjects: LCSH: African Americans—Civil rights—Mississippi—History—20th
century—Juvenile literature. | Civil rights movements—Mississippi—History—20th
century—Juvenile literature. | African American civil rights workers—Mississippi—
History—20th century—Juvenile literature. | African American student movements—
Mississippi—History—20th century—Juvenile literature. | African American youth—
Mississippi—Social conditions—20th century—Juvenile literature. | Mississippi—Race
relations—History—20th century—Juvenile literature.
Classification: LCC E185.93.M6 M275 2021 (print) | LCC E185.93.M6 (ebook)
| DDC 323.1196/0730762—dc23
LC record available at https://lccn.loc.gov/2021001808
LC ebook record available at https://lccn.loc.gov/2021001809

Design by Randall Williams

Printed in the United States of America by Sheridan

The Black Belt, defined by its dark, rich soil, stretches across central Alabama. It was the heart of the cotton belt. It was and is a place of great beauty, of extreme wealth and grinding poverty, of pain and joy. Here we take our stand, listening to the past, looking to the future.

To Noah, Seth, and Katherine

Contents

Foreword

· · · · · · · · · · · ·

Leslie-Burl McLemore

The Mississippi civil rights movement has produced a number of remarkable leaders over the last sixty years. These then young and now much older people blazed a multitude of trails in the state. Most of them emerged from small towns and rural communities. They uniformly grew up in the Black church and many were active in the Youth Councils of the National Association for the Advancement of Colored People (NAACP). In addition, some were members of the Hi-Y and Tri-Hi-Y organizations founded to foster and develop leaders in the Black high schools throughout the state of Mississippi. Of course, some were members of the Future Farmers of America and the 4-H club. Their one commonality was a strong desire to change the status quo in Mississippi.

The young leaders identified in this book were active in the 1950s and 1960s. They were influenced by NAACP field secretary Medgar Wiley Evers, who organized NAACP chapters across Mississippi. Training from Evers and his colleagues taught these young people how to conduct a meeting and organize a protest march. From 1954 to 1963, Evers was the primary civil rights leader in Mississippi. He worked with civil rights organizations and churches throughout the state. He had a reputation for willingness to work with anyone who was dedicated to bringing justice and progress to the State of Mississippi.

The stories of Amos Brown, Johnny Frazier, and Dorie and Joyce Ladner began with their association with Evers in their high schools. Evers worked closely with the NAACP youth councils in the respective communities. Needless to say, the youth council advisors played pivotal roles in the development of young people. The Ladner sisters give tremendous credit to advisor Clyde Kennard in the development of their leadership skills. Kennard went to prison—on a trumped-up charge of stealing chicken feed brought because he had tried to enroll at the University of Southern Mississippi. Amos Brown and Johnny Frazier were also assisted by adult leaders in their communities. Sam Bailey played a major role in working with youth in Jackson. To a person, all would say that they had supportive parents and a favorite teacher or teachers who encouraged them to stand up and speak up for justice and freedom.

The Tougaloo Nine were introduced to Evers after their enrollment at Tougaloo College in Jackson, Mississippi. Author Robert Mayer notes that Evers recruited and trained the Nine to participate in a read-in at the Jackson public library on March 27, 1961. That read-in was one of the first civil rights protests in Mississippi in the 1960s. Of course, we know that students at Jackson's Lanier High School had boycotted the local city buses in the 1940s and that students at Rust College in Holly Springs had boycotted the local segregated movie theater in 1960.

The arrival in Mississippi of the Student Nonviolent Coordinating Committee (SNCC) helped to change the state's civil rights landscape in a profound way. The young SNCC field secretaries went into rural communities and small towns in southwest Mississippi, Jackson, Hattiesburg, and the Mississippi Delta. SNCC ushered in the mass movement in Mississippi, advocating voter registration and direct action. Indeed, SNCC launched a direct action campaign in McComb in 1961. McComb is where we were introduced to Hollis Watkins, Brenda Travis, Curtis Hayes (Muhammad), Billy Talbert, Ike Lewis, and others.

Bob Moses, Marion Barry Jr., Chuck McDew, Reggie Robinson,

Bob Zellner, and other SNCC members came to McComb in the summer of 1961. The SNCC influence helped to elevate the movement to another level. Moses and his colleagues profoundly impacted the young people in McComb and southwest Mississippi. Brenda Travis's heroic story is an example of the courageous leadership demonstrated by young people throughout Mississippi. Travis became the symbol of youth leadership in McComb. Needless to say, the aforementioned young people were at the forefront of the movement.

Robert Mayer's offering is a wonderful introduction to some of those young people who helped to make the Mississippi Movement a reality. The book should encourage all of us to learn more about these young people and the Mississippi movement. It goes without saying that as fascinating as are the stories Mayer has highlighted, he easily could have profiled several other young leaders from the 1950s and 1960s. For instance, the role that Lawrence Guyot of the Mississippi Freedom Democratic Party played, and the on-the-ground efforts of Johnnie Harris, Lee Dilworth, William Scott, Raymond Davis, Rosie Purdy, and many others at Rust College in Holly Springs.

Nonetheless, Mayer has made a major contribution to the literature on the roles of young people in the Mississippi Movement. It is hoped that his contribution will be complemented by stories to come from others with an interest in the fascinating Mississippi story.

Long-time activist Leslie-Burl McLemore was a SNCC field secretary, vice chair of the 1964 Mississippi Freedom Democratic Party's delegation, a city council member and interim mayor of Jackson, a founder of the Fannie Lou Hamer Institute on Citizenship and Democracy, and a professor and interim president of Jackson State University. His doctorate is from the University of Massachusetts (Amherst) and he is also a proud graduate of Mississippi's Rust College.

Some Prefatory Comments

You will see the n-word in this book, maybe more than you care to, so I want to be clear about how and why I include it. When I present the actual word, it will come from the mouth of someone in the past who spoke or wrote the word and hence will always be within a quote. Hearing it may be uncomfortable, but I want you to know how often people used this word and how comfortable they were saying it. I want you to experience the hate-filled world that allowed such a word to exist and be spoken. Maybe if we all understand the historical context of the n-word, we will see its ugly heritage and its use will finally end.

Another term you'll see frequently is "Jim Crow," the name given to the system of segregation that plagued the South from the end of Reconstruction in the 1870s through at least three-fourths of the twentieth century. Though the separation of Blacks and Whites in schools, parks, theaters, and other public places was the hallmark of Jim Crow, the inferiority of Black facilities that were supposed to be "separate but equal" makes clear that the system's real purpose was to mark Black Americans, as a people and as individuals, as inferior to White Americans. The ugly nature of the white supremacy system ran deep and still resonates.

IN 2014 I SPENT three summer weeks in Jackson, Mississippi, living on the campus of Jackson State University and attending a powerful seminar sponsored by the National Endowment for the

Humanities. There I heard noted scholars like Charles M. Payne and John Dittmer, who have studied the Mississippi civil rights movement, and some of the amazing activists like Dorie Ladner and Hollis Watkins who as teenagers plunged into the Mississippi freedom struggle. With freedom fighter Charles McLaurin as our guide, we traveled throughout the state, including the northwest Mississippi Delta counties where some of the most significant events in this book took place.

And we sang freedom songs every day, sometimes led by the great Hollis Watkins, songs he had sung in jail or on marches to keep his spirits up and his fear in check. Through living in Mississippi, I came to know personally some of the geography of the story I will tell and something of the atmosphere where the participants, Black and White, lived. Those three weeks continue to echo in my reflections.

Returning home from Mississippi, I felt compelled to share the history I had encountered face to face. I have done that in these pages.

As I was writing, I thought a great deal about America and about the word "democracy." To some extent, American democracy has been shaped by its leaders—the Abraham Lincolns and the John Adamses. But I also thought a lot about Dr. King and all he stood for and accomplished, about the Dream he shared with us and made our own. Yet he is also only a part of the story.

What then is the other part?

Though Dr. King is among the greatest leaders our country has ever produced, he alone is not the civil rights movement, despite what you might study in school. If we want to talk about the movement and about American democracy, we must speak about the people, the ordinary, everyday people, noble and flawed, who committed and continue to commit to causes larger than themselves.

And here I include the young women and men who laid their lives and futures on the line in a struggle to bring "liberty and justice for all" to their world when those words were so distant from their reality.

This book is about those people, about people who take the core principles of American democracy to heart and hear them as a call; people who believe in the notion of democracy so firmly they are willing to die in the fight; people who are in many ways like us, in other ways not; people who are young and in their early years already coming to understand what it means to fight for ideals, to fight for life.

Why don't we already know much about these kids? I prefer to let you think about that. You are bound to come up with your own unique thoughts.

Why should we know about these kids? Here I will give you my view. Because as a nation we are ill. Because democratic pieces of America are broken. Because Dr. King's dream is still too far from real for too many people of all ages and skin colors and faiths and genders. I'll leave it to you to name what other problems there are, but someone needs to fix them all. Who else but the young? Who else but you?

No "how-to" book will provide the instructions that might help you lead us towards a cure for our national sickness, but there is guidance, there are models for us to follow, heroes to inspire us. So pay attention to the people in these pages. When I do, I learn a great deal.

ACKNOWLEDGMENTS

Judy Smullen edited *In the Name of Emmett Till* and pushed me to think harder about how the book might be shaped to reach a young audience. Beyond appreciating that care and intelligence as an editor, I applaud her good politics and her excellent taste in music.

Michelle Deardorff, Leslie McLemore, Jeff Kolnick, Rico Chapman, Daphne Chamberlain, and Keith Lamont McMillian organized and ran an amazing NEH institute in Jackson, Mississippi, "Finding Mississippi in the National Civil Rights Narrative." My attendance at this institute in 2014 had a profound impact on me. I had been studying Mississippi, but they *showed* me Mississippi and that view pushed me deeper into this book.

Dr. Leslie McLemore again. Dr. McLemore graciously read the manuscript and agreed to write a foreword for the book. I thank him a second time.

Dr. Barry Lee from Morehouse College read the manuscript, offered critique, and wrote a letter of support. In addition, I got to know Dr. Lee during my stay in Jackson where we spent time together eating, talking, and trying to make sense of the world. He generously shared with me and with others details of his life growing up in Indianola, Mississippi. I am grateful for that time spent with Dr. Lee and all he did in support of the book.

My thanks to Naomi Gal for kindly reading and critiquing chapters from the book and Josh Berk for helping me through the arduous task of marketing the book.

I so appreciate working with the great people at NewSouth Books, an important independent press. Suzanne La Rosa warmly brought me into the NewSouth community. Suzanne and Matthew Byrne guided me through the publication process with a kind, thoughtful spirit. I learned so much from Randall Williams as he did final editing. I am amazed at Randall's knowledge, skill, kindness, and wisdom. May publishers like NewSouth thrive.

Then there is Jan, who graciously listens to me babble on about Mississippi, as well as other topics I write about, and loves me just the same. So much to be thankful for.

Abbreviations and Glossary

CORE   Congress of Racial Equality
COFO   Council of Federated Organizations
FBI   Federal Bureau of Investigation
FOR   Fellowship of Reconciliation
ICC   Interstate Commerce Commission
KKK   Ku Klux Klan
MFDP Mississippi Freedom Democratic Party
NAACP National Association for the Advancement of Colored People
SCLC   Southern Christian Leadership Council
SNCC Student Nonviolent Coordinating Committee
WCC   White Citizens' Councils

Civil Rights Act of 1964 — The federal law that legally ended segregation in public facilities and banned other forms of discrimination.

Congress of Racial Equality — A civil rights organization founded in 1942 and grounded in the philosophy of nonviolence as taught by the Indian leader Mahatma Mohandas Gandhi.

Council of Federated Organizations — A Mississippi umbrella organization formed to coordinate the activities in the state of all organizations working for civil rights from 1961 to 1965.

Freedom Rides — Direct action protests in 1961 to end segregation in interstate transportation, such as buses and trains, and within depots and terminals.

Freedom Schools — Created by SNCC in 1964 as a part of Freedom Summer, these progressive schools provided an alternative to the segregated, underfunded education provided to African Americans in the South, particularly in rural areas.

Freedom Summer — A large-scale 1964 project bringing Northern and White college students to Mississippi to focus national attention on civil rights activities, including voter registration and education.

Interstate Commerce Commission — The federal agency that regulates commerce and transportation between the states and thus ruled that segregation on buses, trains, and airplanes was illegal.

Jim Crow — The system of laws and customs that segregated, demeaned, and discriminated against Blacks in the interest of white supremacy.

Ku Klux Klan — A violent, secretive white supremacist organization begun by ex-Confederates after the Civil War to restore white control in the South. The KKK reemerged in the 1920s against immigration and again in the 1950s–1960s against the civil rights movement.

Literacy tests — Questions and exams used in the South by White authorities to disqualify Black applicants from registering to vote. Voting officials were given wide latitude to decide who failed, allowing the officials generally to pass Whites and reject Blacks.

Mississippi Freedom Democratic Party — An independent political party created in 1964 to challenge the then all-White Mississippi Democratic Party.

Mississippi Sovereignty Commission — A state spy agency operating from 1956 to 1977 to gather intelligence on anyone involved in the civil rights movement or sympathetic to desegregation. The agency compiled dossiers on 87,000 people.

National Association for the Advancement of Colored People — An organization established in 1909 to promote equality, eliminate prejudice, advance the interest of "colored citizens," and seek justice in the courts, schools, and workplace. The NAACP strategy was focused on litigation and legislation. During the 1960s in Mississippi and under the leadership of Medgar Evers, the NAACP employed more direct action.

Reconstruction — The period following the Civil War when the 13th, 14th, and 15 amendments to the U.S. Constitution were adopted, abolishing slavery, extending citizenship, and guaranteeing the vote, particularly in the former Confederate states. The effort foundered when Southern whites regained control of the region's political offices, often by fraud, intimidation, and violence.

Sharecropping — A post-slavery system of farming in which mostly White and wealthy landowners provided land, seed, and equipment to poor and mostly Black farmers. Sharecroppers provided their labor and received a share of the crop they themselves produced, just enough to keep them poor and in constant debt.

Student Nonviolent Coordinating Committee — An organization of mostly young people that began in April 1960 following the first sit-ins in Greensboro, North Carolina, and Nashville, Tennessee, and then spread throughout the South. The initial SNCC activists were male and female, white and black, Southern and Northern. SNCC was more activist than the older civil rights organizations. It dissolved about 1968.

Voting Rights Act of 1965 — A federal law passed in response to official White discrimination, intimidation, and fraud used to prevent African Americans from registering to vote and fairly casting ballots at the state and local levels. The new law essentially enforced the Fifteenth Amendment.

White Citizens' Councils — This segregationist organization formed in Mississippi after *Brown v. Board of Education* and spread to chapters across the Deep South from 1954 into the 1970s. It was a sort of white-collar KKK. Its members disavowed violence but used intimidation, social and economic pressure, and

White-controlled governments to block or at least delay school and social integration.

White supremacy — A belief that Whites are inherently superior to Blacks and should legally and socially be under White control and domination.

Timeline

· · · · · · · · · · ·

1954

May 17	*Brown v. Board of Education* decision handed down
December 15	Medgar Evers becomes assistant field secretary for the Mississippi branch of the NAACP

1955

May 7	George Lee assassinated
August 28	Emmett Till murdered
September 3	Emmett Till's funeral
September 19–23	J. W. Milam and Roy Bryant acquitted of Till's murder
December 1	Rosa Parks arrested for violating bus segregation laws
December 5	Montgomery Bus Boycott begins

1956

Spring	Amos Brown becomes president of NAACP's West Jackson Youth Council
December 21	Montgomery Bus Boycott ends in success

1958

Summer	Amos Brown speaks out against segregated schools; almost gets expelled from high school

1960

February 1	Four students sit in at Woolworth's in Greensboro, North Carolina
April	SNCC founded at Shaw University
May	Johnny Frazier kicked out of high school
August	Johnny Frazier beaten in a Winona jail cell

1961

March 27	Tougaloo Nine sit in at Jackson public library
March 29	Tougaloo Nine convicted and given suspended sentences; Jackson State College march in support

May-August	First cycle of Freedom Rides
June	Amos Brown and others sit in at the Jackson zoo
July 6	Hezekiah Watkins enters Greyhound station in Jackson, is arrested, sent to Parchman Farm
July 11	Luvaughn Brown and Jimmie Travis sit in at Walgreens lunch counter in Jackson
Mid-July	Robert Moses comes to McComb
Late August	Hollis Watkins and Curtis Hayes (Muhammed) sit in at the Woolworth's in McComb
	Brenda Travis, Ike Lewis, and Robert Talbot sit in at the McComb Greyhound station
September 22	ICC orders end to segregated interstate transportation
October	Segregated state fair boycotted in Jackson
October 4	Burglund High School students walk out
November 1	September ICC ruling goes into effect
November 29	Freedom Riders integrate McComb Greyhound station
December 1	More Freedom Riders integrate McComb Greyhound station
December 2	Three expelled Burglund High students integrate McComb Greyhound station

1962

June 18	Sam Block comes to Greenwood
June-July	SNCC sponsors first mass meetings in Greenwood to discuss voter registration
Early August	Sam Block starts to bring people to the courthouse to register
August 16	Luvaughn Brown and Lawrence Guyot join Sam Block; the SNCC office is attacked
August	Fannie Lou Hamer attempts to register to vote; she is fired and thrown off the plantation where she works
October	Young people boycott segregated state fair in Jackson
October	Leflore County Board of Supervisors vote to suspend distribution of food provided by the federal government
October 1	James Meredith desegregates University of Mississippi
Winter	SNCC begins food drive to feed the people of Greenwood
December	Jackson's Black community boycotts downtown stores Six are arrested picketing at Woolworth's

1963

February 20	Four buildings near SNCC office in Greenwood burned

February 28	Gunmen shoot at SNCC car striking Jimmie Travis
March to April	The Greenwood movement flowers with SNCC organizers, mass meetings, and attempts to register to vote
March 26–27	Shots fired at home of Dewey Greene Sr.; march in Greenwood occurs the next day
March 29	Rev. Tucker is bitten by a police dog during a march taking place after voting registration efforts in Greenwood.
April–May	Marches and violence in Birmingham
May 28	Activists sit in at Woolworth's in Jackson
May 30	Students walkout at Lanier High School in Jackson
May 31	Children's March takes place in Jackson
Summer	Anne Moody comes to Canton
June	CORE's George Raymond comes to Canton
June 9	June Johnson, Fannie Lou Hamer, and other activists beaten in Winona, Mississippi
June 11	President Kennedy addresses the nation about civil rights
June 12	Medgar Evers assassinated by Byron De La Beckwith
June 15	Processional for Medgar Evers spirals into near riot
August 28	March on Washington for Jobs and Freedom
September 15	Birmingham's 16th Street Baptist Church bombed

1964

January	CORE starts boycott of stores in Canton
February 28	First Canton Freedom Day
March 2	Canton students boycott schools
March	Freedom School curriculum conference in New York City
March 13	Second Canton Freedom Day
May 29	Third Canton Freedom Day
June 14–27	Freedom Summer volunteers oriented in Oxford, Ohio
June–August	Freedom Summer takes place
June 21	CORE's Chaney, Goodman, and Schwerner murdered
July	Freedom Schools open
July 2	President Johnson signs the Civil Rights Act of 1964
July 5–July 25	McGhee brothers sit in at Greenwood's Leflore Theatre
August 15	Silas McGhee shot in Greenwood
August 22	Fannie Lou Hamer speaks to the DNC in Atlantic City

1965

August 6	President Johnson signs the Voting Rights Act of 1965

In the Name of Emmett Till

1   Emmett Till: The Beginning

"THE WORST BEATING I EVER SAW"

The young fisherman stepped into his motorboat, headed out into the water, checked the trotline he had stretched across the muddy Tallahatchie River, looked across, and noticed something terrifying. He later told a court, "I seen two knees and feet." The seventeen-year-old, Robert Hodges, first checked other lines he had set and then went home to tell his father what he saw.

Later, a group of men returned with Robert to the river. They floated out in two boats and dragged a body to shore.

This wasn't easy. As the men pulled the corpse from the water, Hodges saw barbed wire wrapped around its neck. And someone had attached the other end of the wire to a seventy-five pound cotton gin fan to weigh the body down. Describing what he saw, Hodges later testified, "It was beaten pretty bad in the back . . . and hips." The head ". . . was also gashed in on the side."

The sheriff arrived a little later in the morning. When he examined the body he saw a bullet hole "above the right ear" and that "the left side of his face had been cut up or beat up, plumb into the skull." Someone had gouged out one of his eyes. Another police officer stated flatly it was "the worst beating I ever saw."

Though Hodges did not yet know it, he learned later that the mutilated body was that of a fourteen-year-old boy named Emmett Louis Till.

Emmett's great-uncle, Mose Wright, came to identify the

deceased. Horrified by what had been done to Emmett, he thought about his nephew's innocence and sweetness: "There was Bobo who used to have such a good appetite and who never sassed in my house, not once. There he was dead, looking like he had been hit with a sledgehammer."

EMMETT COMES TO MISSISSIPPI

Just months previously Emmett, known to his family as "Bo" and "Bobo," begged his mother, Mamie Till-Mobley (she was widowed and remarried), to let him make the trip from Chicago to Mississippi. A vacation would be a two-week break from the noise and congestion of the city—a chance to spend time with cousins and an opportunity to fish.

Once Mrs. Till-Mobley gave in to her son, she sat Bo down and had "the talk": "I emphasized over and over again to him that [Mississippi] was not the same as . . . Chicago and he had to be

Emmett Till with his mother, Mrs. Mamie Till-Mobley.

extra careful to avoid getting in trouble with White people." Born in the Mississippi Delta, Till-Mobley knew the unwritten "code of behavior" and warned Emmett about following the rules necessary for Black survival in Mississippi: don't just say "yes" to White people, say "Yes, sir" and "Yes, ma'am"; when a White person is coming at you on the sidewalk, step aside and keep your eyes down; never look back at a White woman after she has passed.

Being young, innocent, and playful, Emmett needed the talk. He brought that playful nature to Mississippi. His cousin Curtis Jones described him as "the type of guy [who] loved fun and jokes, he loved to play a joke on people for some laugh, he laughed all the time, . . . we went fishing in a little mudhole down there. And, I'm fishing and all of a sudden I hear some water flash. And he'd throwed a log in the water, and said, 'That was a big fish just jump up over there,' you know. And he'd break out and laugh." Till-Mobley added, "Bo was liked by everybody."

Emmett stood five foot three inches but he weighed one hundred and sixty pounds, big for a fourteen-year-old. He had brown hair and hazel eyes. At the age of three, a bout with polio left him with a stutter, but with his mom's help he had mostly overcome it. It only seemed to return when he got nervous, so his mother taught him to purse his lips at those nervous times, in effect to whistle.

At Bryant's Grocery

In late August 1955, Emmett rode the train from Chicago to Mississippi, traveling with his great-uncle, Mose Wright, and his cousin Wheeler Parker. Arriving in Mississippi, Emmett quickly learned the feel of Southern life. At night he stayed with his cousins at the Wrights' home near Greenwood, a small city on the eastern edge of the Mississippi Delta. During the day he picked cotton, finding the work arduous.

Around 8 p.m. on August 24, the fourth day of his visit, Emmett and his cousins drove about three miles west to a small country grocery store in Money, Mississippi, a crossroads, not even a town, in an area just outside Greenwood along the Tallahatchie River.

As the car pulled up, some boys were playing checkers on the porch. Emmett and his cousins also sat down and started talking. Emmett may have shown the others pictures of his friends from Chicago, including a picture of a White girl. Someone told Emmett there was a "pretty lady" working in the store and encouraged him to go inside to take a look. Soon, Emmett went into the store to buy some bubblegum.

But he forgot his mother's warnings.

Twenty-one-year-old Carolyn Bryant, the wife of the store's owner, sat behind the counter. She was just five feet two inches tall, and she weighed only 103 pounds. She was little, but a gun she kept under the seat of her car made up for her stature.

We do not know exactly what happened in the store that day. Emmett was alone with Mrs. Bryant for around a minute, perhaps just a little longer. He may have touched Mrs. Bryant and jokingly asked her for a date. He may have placed the money for the bubblegum in her hand instead of placing it on the counter. If he placed the money in her hand, he was breaking the rules of behavior between the races that his mom had warned him about.

A cousin came in to watch over Emmett. Bo paid for the items and went outside. On the way out he waved and called out "Goodbye," without a "Ma'am" as the unwritten code of conduct required.

At the later trial, Carolyn Bryant told a very unlikely story, insisting that Emmett had placed his hand on hers, had asked her for a date, and then had placed his arm around her waist. [She has recently admitted that she lied.]

You can see there are different versions of this story.

Outside again, as the boys watched Carolyn Bryant walk down the store's ramp and head to her car, Emmett let out a long wolf whistle that terrified the cousins. According to cousin Simeon Wright, "It was a loud wolf whistle, a big-city 'whee wheeeee!' and it caught us all by surprise." Till-Mobley wondered later if the whistle wasn't just Emmett being nervous, trying to form words, and whistling as his mother had instructed him to do. Simeon claimed that Bo "was just trying to be funny." At any rate, someone shouted "She's getting a gun!" and the boys jumped in their car and sped away, laughing about their scare. They hoped the whole thing would blow over, but word got around.

THE MURDER

Less than a week later, Roy Bryant (Carolyn's husband) and his half-brother, J. W. Milam, and probably others, showed up at the Wright home. It was Sunday around 2 a.m. when Bryant and Milam burst past Mose Wright and into the house. Brandishing a flashlight and gun, the men searched the small residence, quickly finding Emmett and demanding that he get dressed and come with them. Mrs. Wright pleaded for Emmett but to no avail. On the way out, Milam threatened Wright, ordering him to tell no one, and hauled Emmett away.

Again, we have conflicting accounts of what happened next, but we do know that Emmett was brutally beaten and shot and his body was dumped into the Tallahatchie River.

After three days with no sign of Emmett, Wright went to the county sheriff. In response, the sheriff questioned Bryant and Milam, finally arresting them on September 6 for kidnapping. After Robert Hodges found Emmett's body, the sheriff upped the charge to murder. The trial of the two men took place from Monday, September 19, to Friday, September 23, in the Tallahatchie County Courthouse in Sumner, Mississippi, the county where the body was found.

THE TRIAL

That September, temperatures in Mississippi rose to the mid-nineties, accompanied by stifling humidity. The courtroom—built for one hundred and fifty persons and without air-conditioning—filled with three hundred spectators.

Reporters from both Black and White newspapers attended, as did news people from the three TV networks, ABC, NBC, and CBS. Though local sheriff Clarence Strider disdained the presence of Black journalists in the courtroom and announced, "I ain't having no nigger reporters in my courtroom," Judge Curtis Swango Jr. overruled him, allowing the Black writers in, although they had to sit in a segregated area in the back, crowded around a small card table. Sheriff Strider found other ways to share his ugly feelings. He greeted the Black press every day with, "Good morning, niggers."

The atmosphere in the courtroom was informal, even a little festive, with the judge popping open a soda bottle on the first day and spectators joining him, some with beer. Hawkers roamed the courtroom selling sodas and box lunches. According to Simeon Booker, reporting for *Jet* magazine, "J. W. Milam smoked cigars and read newspapers during the proceedings. He seemed bored with it all."

The trial began on Monday with jury selection. The jury included only White men.

On Wednesday prosecutors questioned the first witness, Mose Wright, who testified about the night of his nephew's abduction. He explained that at 2 a.m. two men came to his door, one calling out "Preacher, Preacher." Wright said he recognized J. W. Milam's voice. Soon the prosecutor requested, "Now stop there a minute, Uncle Mose, I want you to point out Mr. Milam if you see him there." Wright stood, looked around the courtroom, pointed at Milam, and exclaimed, "There he is." The prosecutor then asked Wright to

The all-white male jury deciding the fate of Till's murderers, Roy Bryant and J. W. Milam.

identify the person with Milam that night, and he pointed at Roy Bryant. Wright stated that Milam asked him if he had "two boys there from Chicago" and he responded, "Yes, Sir."

For that courageous testimony, Mose Wright had to fear for his life. He had broken one of Mississippi's unwritten rules: Black men did not publicly accuse White men of crimes. Not long after, he fled the state.

Later in the trial, eighteen-year-old Willie Reed testified that he saw Emmett in the bed of a pickup truck at 6 a.m. with some other people. (In 1955, Milam and Bryant were the only suspected killers. Today it is believed that many more were involved.) Reed could identify only Milam as one of those with Emmett.

Apparently the men guarding Emmett hauled him off the truck and into a large shed. Reed testified that he saw them all go into the shed from which Reed heard "a whole lot of licks" from a beating and then cries, wails, shouts of "Mama, please save me" and "Please, God, don't do it again." The assault went on for an hour. Eventually the crying out ceased.

What goes on in the mind of men so cruel, men somehow able to beat a fourteen-year old boy, listening to his pleas?

At one point during the ordeal, Reed saw Milam emerge from the shed, pistol in his holster, followed not long after by some men rolling a tarp with something wrapped in it onto the pickup truck. Was that Emmett's body? Reed testified that he then watched as some of those men started a fire and burned some clothes.

For his testimony, Reed also had to sneak out of the state. His violation of unwritten codes stating Blacks did not accuse Whites of crimes was a behavior condemned at the time more harshly in White Mississippi than the murder of a Black boy.

The murderers then evidently took Emmett's body to the Tallahatchie River where they weighted it down with barbed wire attached to the cotton gin fan and dumped it.

Other potential witnesses were not available to testify. Not only had Sheriff Strider done zero investigative work to help the prosecution of Milam and Bryant, he had arrested two potential Black witnesses and detained them in a nearby prison so they could not testify. A Southern sheriff in those days could always find an excuse to arrest a Black person. Given the power of the testimony from Wright and Reed, you can see why the sheriff thought such an action was a good idea.

On Thursday, Emmett's mother, having traveled from Chicago, testified that the mutilated body that had come back to her was that of her son.

In their summation the next day, the lawyer for the defense told the jury he was certain "that every last Anglo-Saxon one of you has the courage to free these men." Another attorney told them, "your forefathers will turn over in their graves" if Milam and Bryant were found guilty.

On Friday, after deliberating for only sixty-seven minutes, the jury declared Bryant and Milam not guilty of murder. The White crowd in the courtroom cheered. Later, swarmed by reporters and friends, Bryant and Milam lit cigars in celebration and kissed their wives on cue for the camera.

In November, to no one's surprise, an all-White grand jury chose not to indict Milam and Bryant for kidnapping.

Two months later, speaking to a reporter from *Look* magazine, a national publication with nearly four million subscribers, Bryant and Milam described in detail what they had done to Emmett and confessed that they had murdered him. But Milam offered what he believed was a rational justification for his crime:

> Well, what else could we do? He was hopeless. I'm no bully; I never hurt a nigger in my life. I like niggers—in their place—I know how to work 'em. But I just decided it was time a few people got put on notice. As long as I live and can do anything about it, niggers are gonna stay in their place. Niggers ain't gonna vote where I live. If they did, they'd control the government. They ain't gonna go to school with my kids. And when a nigger gets close to mentioning sex with a White woman, he's tired o' livin'. I'm likely to kill him.

Though today some important details of the *Look* story are in dispute, the confession itself is not.

Perhaps Emmett Till was destined to become one more Black person killed because he overstepped the White boundaries that fenced him in, killed because he did not or would not play by the unwritten rules, killed simply because he was Black in a world of cruel white supremacy. In that Jim Crow (see Glossary) world, such murders went unnoticed beyond the local Black community.

Emmett's mom would see to it that such obscurity would not come to be for her son.

"LET THE WORLD SEE WHAT THEY DID TO MY BOY!"

When Mamie Till-Mobley got word about the murder and the fact that Sheriff Clarence Strider hoped to bury Emmett quickly in Mississippi, she protested loudly and demanded that her son's body be sent back to Chicago. On September 2, when a train with the body arrived, Emmett's mother went to the station to make sure the body was indeed Emmett's. With her were one thousand people who had heard of Emmett's lynching from local Black newspapers. Opening the casket, Till-Mobley collapsed in horror at what she saw, but later she insisted that Emmett's casket be open during visitation and the funeral, exclaiming, "Let the world see what they did to my boy!"

For four days, that casket remained open in the funeral home with Emmett's mutilated body on display. Two hundred and fifty thousand people came to pay their respects. According to Simeon Booker, "Many fainted. Some screamed. So many eyes wept." At the funeral on September 6, several thousand sat inside while five thousand more waited outside. *Jet* magazine published a picture of Emmett's brutalized body.

Mamie Till-Mobley did not rest, making sure that the world knew about her son's murder. She spoke about Emmett and his lynching wherever she could. In Cleveland she told a crowd, "The murder of my son has shown me that what happens to any of us, anywhere in the world, had better be the business of us all."

Young people everywhere paid attention, especially in the South.

Young Mississippian Joyce Ladner later became a member of the Student Nonviolent Coordinating Committee (SNCC). She recalled, "Ours was the Emmett Till generation. No other single incident had a more profound effect on so many people who came into SNCC. We had seen the *Jet* magazine cover of Emmett Till's disfigured and bloated face with one eye missing. . . . We were his age and could identify with him. . . . The image is with me still.

It became etched in my generation's consciousness."

As a result of Emmett Till's brutal murder and the exoneration of his murderers, the Black community throughout the nation was outraged. That outrage was particularly motivating to young people like Joyce Ladner, her sister Dorie, and the members of a group that would come to be known as the "Tougaloo Nine" who remembered Emmett Till as they dared to sit in at a public library they were forbidden to enter. It was also a stimulus to action by a person who would become their mentor and one of Mississippi's most important leaders, Medgar Evers.

Elders I—Medgar Evers
Joins the Fight for Freedom

. . . .

FIGHTING FOR FREEDOM ABROAD

During World War II, not long after D-Day, Medgar Evers landed on the beaches of Normandy to participate in the brutal fighting that ended the Nazi dream of global domination. Evers had enlisted and risen to the rank of sergeant in one of those segregated Black regiments that mirrored a segregated America that fought German racists in Europe while ignoring the racism at home. After two and a half years in the army, Evers came back to Mississippi with two combat stars.

He also came back with a new view of how the world should be, even though serving his country overseas had changed nothing for his or any other Black person's circumstances in the South. On his return to Mississippi, he rode home sitting in the back of a bus. His sister Elizabeth reported, "He had to go all the way to the back of the bus and sit down with his army uniform on—[after he] don' went and fought for his country." With that bus ride as just one more humiliation, Evers decided to fight again for what was right, this time on the home front.

GROWING UP WITH HATE, FIGHTING FOR FREEDOM

The bigotry Evers experienced in the U.S. Army was nothing new to him. He recalled growing up in Decatur, Mississippi, with a White playmate who "practically lived at my house." The two "would do all the things that kids do—play hide and seek, talk about our big plans for growing up, swap the little personal treasures that boys grow friendly over, and argue over his double-barreled stopper gun." Then something happened. The friend no longer came around, and young Medgar did not understand why.

One day he saw the boy standing out in the street with a group of other White kids. The boy called him "nigger." Later Evers said, "I guess at that moment I realized my status in Mississippi. I have lived with it ever since."

After the war, his battle on the homefront beginning, Evers first thought deeply about what to fight for and decided on voting—the most fundamental democratic right, a right denied to most African Americans in Mississippi and throughout the South since the days of Reconstruction and denied to all Blacks in Decatur.

In 1946, Evers, his brother Charles, and four others headed to the Newton County Courthouse in Decatur to register to vote, as other Black G.I.'s throughout the South did. Though the six men registered successfully, on the day of the primary—the day when they went to actually vote—they hit a brick wall.

As they approached, the registrar stepped up to ask the six to come into his office where they found themselves surrounded by twenty White men who voiced vicious threats if they dared persist in exercising their right to vote. Charles remembered, "Man it was rednecks everywhere. They . . . had guns and baseball bats." One man told him, "Nigger, you better go'n back and get on out before you get hurt."

Medgar and Charles knew these men, many of them childhood friends. Amongst them Charles saw Dr. Jack, the doctor who had delivered both of the Evers boys. When Charles asked the doctor how he could deny them the right to the vote, Dr. Jack told him, "Well, but see, some things you niggers ain't supposed to do."

As Medgar and his comrades walked home, the Whites followed in cars, one guy leaning out of the window with a shotgun ". . . keeping a bead on us all the time . . ."

The six young men did not vote that day. But this failure ignited Evers's fight.

LEADER OF THE NAACP

In 1948 Evers enrolled at Alcorn College (now Alcorn State University), a historically Black school across the state from Decatur. He completed his degree in 1952 and became an insurance sales-man. His job taught him something important that he would use later as an activist: you must connect in some personal way with the people you hope to influence. His travels around the Delta meeting customers and making those connections also brought him face to face with the terrible living conditions Black sharecroppers were subject to. More about this later.

Deciding he could advance Black freedom better as an attorney, Evers sought to attend law school at "Ole Miss" —the University of Mississippi—but the segregated school would not admit him. So, in 1954, he sought assistance from the NAACP (National As-sociation for the Advancement of Colored People), the national organization that filed lawsuits when Blacks were discriminated against. Ole Miss still denied his application and would stay segre-gated until 1962 when James Meredith's court-ordered admission led to White rioting, two deaths, and the imposition of martial law by the Kennedy administration.

Through that battle, the NAACP leadership came to know Medgar Evers, and they were impressed. Roy Wilkins, national head of the NAACP, offered Evers a job as an assistant field secretary in Mississippi. Evers did not have to think long. He quickly accepted, quitting his insurance job and starting his new career officially on December 15, 1954. After organizing several successful branches of the NAACP in Mississippi, first in Mound Bayou and then in Cleveland, he soon became field secretary for the entire state.

Evers had served as field secretary for less than a year when Emmett Till was murdered. Evers reacted to the lynching as the father he was. His wife, Myrlie, whom Medgar had met and married while both were students at Alcorn and with whom he had three children, later recalled, "Medgar cried when he found that this happened to Emmett Till." Since Sheriff Strider had no interest in pursuing the truth, the job of finding witnesses and evidence fell to Evers and others in the NAACP.

So Evers and several colleagues went to work. To gather evidence, Evers disguised himself as a sharecropper, wearing "overalls and beat-up shoes" and going out into the Delta cotton fields to speak with people who might know something about the murder. He knew that if White people knew what he was doing he likely would have been beaten or worse. Beyond investigating, Evers worked hard to spread the word about what had happened to Emmett.

Sadly, Evers often found himself investigating the murders of African Americans in Mississippi.

As field secretary, a post he held until his death, Evers traveled the state. Just as he had done as an insurance salesman, he went door-to-door so he could meet with people directly and invite them to come to meetings to hear him speak about all the ways the community could fight for long-denied civil rights.

A warm, caring, committed individual who connected with everyone in the community, Evers drew lots of people into the movement, but his greatest success was with young people, so hungry for a better life. He was especially proud of his work organizing NAACP youth chapters. Evers spoke honestly and courageously to the young; they responded in kind.

A TRIBUTE

The Reverend Shirley Harrington, an activist from Jackson, Mississippi, first heard Medgar Evers when she was thirteen:

> One of the things I can remember was standing on my tiptoes at Mt. Helm Baptist Church . . . trying to see this man. He spoke with the voice of authority. His demeanor was so sure. His words were eloquent. And his tenacity was above anything I had ever seen.
>
> There were people in every corner of the building. There were other children. I was one of the youngest. As he began to tell us what economic empowerment would mean, what voter registration would mean, what having schools that were not desegregated or segregated but were open to all. I couldn't believe it.
>
> And what was so amazing was, he was a member of our neighborhood. He lived in Shady Oak. He and my father were members of the same lodge, right across the street. He had little children too . . .
>
> He soon became my hero. He became a role model. I aspired to speak like him. I wanted to have the same kind of dedication and vision that he had.
>
> And so in just a few hours, I was a convert in the Jackson civil rights movement. That trail of meetings every week from one church to another would educate us, inspire us, and give us its vision. A vision of no more discrimination. No more separate schools. No more going to downtown Jackson and not being able to try on clothes, no more Colored water, no more Colored restrooms. And I could see the vision at thirteen.

2 The Tougaloo Nine and the Ladner Sisters

· ·

THE LADNER SISTERS

Even the young experienced the sickness of Jim Crow segregation as a part of their day-to-day lives. Some fought back.

When Dorie Ladner was around thirteen, she and her sister Joyce headed over to the local White-owned grocery store for treats. The store stood one block from their home. After Dorie picked out a doughnut and handed her money to the cashier, the girls strolled over to the rack and looked at magazines. The White cashier crept over, skulking behind them. According to Joyce, he tried to place his hands on Dorie's breasts, but Dorie "turned around, took the bag of doughnuts, and began to beat him over the head!" They fled home, fearing what their mother would say. When Dorie explained to her mother what had happened, Mrs. Ladner told her daughter, "You should have killed him. Don't ever let any White man touch you wrong."

With no legal recourse and facing severe retaliation if they spoke up, African American women in the South often just put up with the sexual abuse that came with the Jim Crow system. But the Ladner girls learned to do more than endure, lessons that began with their mother who instructed her daughters to stand up for themselves: "Never allow anyone to push you around."

"When we were very young," four or five as Dorie recalls, "I remember her telling us to always look a White man in the eyes when you're talking and"— Joyce finished her sister's sentence— "And don't blink!" Over and over Mrs. Ladner reminded the girls that they "were as good as anybody."

Taking that assurance from their mother, they expanded their minds further so that they could understand the world and discover how they could fight a mean system. Though the Ladners grew up in Palmer's Crossing, the remote Black section of Hattiesburg, Mississippi, they managed to read widely, gleaning news about the realities of African American life throughout the country. An adult cousin introduced the young girls to Black newspapers like the *Pittsburgh Courier* and *Chicago Defender* and magazines published for the African American community such as *Jet* and *Ebony*. He also brought them books about Black life. As the sisters studied these sources and learned about their world, they imagined possibilities and prepared to act. As Joyce said, ". . . that outside information just fueled our curiosity and fed it and made us want to see the world and do things differently."

LYNCHINGS

One particular story captured the girls' attention—the lynching of Emmett Till. After they heard what had happened, Joyce made sure to be at the grocery store every afternoon at 4:20 when a city bus dropped off the local newspaper she could buy for a dime. She carried it home and clipped out every article about the murder, creating a scrapbook. She read every word she could find about Emmett Till. For Dorie, stories like his, all too common, pushed her to become a better scholar, asking her social studies teacher to explain the thirteenth, fourteenth, and fifteenth amendments, studying the Constitution, and memorizing its preamble.

What must it have been like for the two young girls to confront the lynching of a kid just like them? Joyce was thirteen when he was killed, and Dorie was fourteen, the same age as Emmett.

One thing is for sure: the horror of the murder and the subsequent contemptuous lack of justice fueled a determination inside both sisters. At fourteen Dorie knew to ask the most powerful question about the murderers: ". . . if these men are guilty, then why aren't they being punished?" Joyce likely spoke for both of them when she remembers, ". . . just feeling tremendously powerless, . . . I would sort of sit and dream about one day." Joyce later referred to herself and other young activists as "the Emmett Till generation."

And then in 1959, four years after Till's death, this time just twenty miles from Palmer's Crossing, it happened again. Mack Charles Parker, a young Black man of twenty-three, sat in jail, accused of raping a White woman. Everyone in the community felt Parker would easily win his case because his lawyer had evidence that would prove his innocence. The trial never happened. Instead, a White mob burst into the jail, abducted Parker, took him across the state line into Louisiana, shot him, and then tossed his body off a bridge into the Pearl River.

The two killings fit frighteningly into a world Joyce recognized, a world where, after Parker's lynching, she heard comments on the street such as, "They should've killed that nigger. I wish I'd been there. I would've done whatever to him. I would've kicked him, too, or I would've gotten me a shot on him."

The girls were again crushed, feeling "just really angry" —and wanting so much to take some action, do something to fight back against a system that could allow such injustice. So they did.

THE LADNERS AND MEDGAR EVERS

Still just teenaged kids in high school, the two organized a youth chapter of the NAACP in Palmer's Crossing. They met Medgar Evers, attended state conferences up the road in Jackson, Mississippi, and worked actively with local civil rights leaders. When their mentor, Clyde Kennard, was falsely accused of theft—$25 worth of chicken feed—and sentenced to seven years in a high-security prison, the sisters launched a campaign to gain his release. As Joyce said: "We were little girls who were interested in Negro rights, as they were called."

After graduating from high school in 1960, the Ladners attended Jackson State, a historically Black college in Jackson. They arrived as seasoned and highly committed activists, but administrators at Jackson State discouraged protest in their students, so a showdown was in the works.

Early on the sisters learned how to skirt restrictions on student behavior. So on Wednesday afternoons when students did not have classes, they signed out of their dormitory stating they planned "to go downtown to shop," but instead they marched down the street to the NAACP headquarters for meetings with Evers. If anyone at the college found out, the girls would have been in trouble. In fact, they didn't stay out of trouble for long!

Dorie and Joyce paid attention as students at nearby Tougaloo College, a historically Black private liberal arts school founded just after the Civil War by northern missionaries, prepared an important challenge to Jim Crow segregation. This was the sort of audacious confrontation rarely seen in Mississippi in those days, but Tougaloo's faculty and administration was ready to support activism and the student body was eager to fight for civil rights.

THE TOUGALOO NINE DECIDE TO ACT

Nine Tougaloo students knew they were literally putting their lives on the line that day in the spring of 1961. As Al Lassiter, one of the Nine, acknowledged many years later, "I thought I might get hurt, possibly killed, but if you were concentrating on your personal safety, you probably wouldn't have gone." The action that might have gotten Al Lassiter killed? Entering a public library and sitting down to read a book.

What possessed them?

Geraldine Edwards Hollis had a simple, clear reason: "Reading was my passion. I was one of those people who read under the blanket with a flashlight. So when they mentioned that we might want to go to the library, I was ready," she recalled.

James Bradford, another member of the Tougaloo Nine, remembered one night when he was thirteen. Having just run an errand for his mother, he got on the bus and, without thinking, sat down in front of a White man. When he realized what he had done, "unlike Rosa Parks I popped up like something stuck me. I got up and went to the back of the bus which was my place—but I hated it." The memory motivated him to become one of the Nine .

The students who made up the Nine had already thought a lot about injustice, having joined an NAACP Youth Council and fallen under the sway of Evers and Tougaloo campus chaplain John Mangram. They came up with the idea of the sit-in and studied effective nonviolent action. With Evers and Mangram as advisors, the students carefully planned each step of what they would do.

THE READ-IN

Early on the morning of Monday, March 27, 1961, the nine students traveled first to the George Washington Carver branch of the public library, the "Colored library," a facility small and woefully inferior to the local libraries established for Whites. The students were nicely dressed, the young women in skirts and the young men in coats and ties.

They went in and asked for certain books, knowing already that those books wouldn't be in the small collection. Alfred Cook, a biology major, asked for *Introduction to Parasitology*, a rare microbiology book that he needed. No one could supply the materials the students requested, and they moved on.

At 11 a.m. the students arrived at the main branch of the Jackson

Library on State Street, just down from the state capitol. As they crossed the street together, they experienced an onslaught of media. According to Bradford, "When we got out of the cars the media was there. They popped out of the bushes or wherever they had been hiding, and the cameras started to roll." The students, working with their mentor Evers, had informed the press in advance. They hoped to generate publicity and to lessen the chances of brutality at the hands of the authorities they knew would be coming. The press followed the students into the library.

One student went straight for the card catalog and located the books he needed, the ones not available at the Carver Library. Others took books from the shelves and sat down to read at tables situated throughout the library. The White librarian and the few White patrons in the library that day looked surprised to see the young Black people. Joseph Jackson recalled, "When I saw the expression of those faces on those White people, I mean it was a hush. Just looking at the expression; they were frightened."

The White folks were not the only ones who were afraid.

Once Ethel Sawyer had taken her book off the shelf and sat down at a table, she looked out the window and saw a "menacing-looking" crowd gathering outside, some "shaking their fists." She later said, "I remember being nervous. And I remember thinking, I sure hope the police will hurry up and get here." Later Sawyer noticed that the book she was "reading" was upside down.

The librarian approached the students and asked why they had come. One explained they were gathering materials for their college research. She told them to go back to Carver library, their library, and order the books they wanted from the main branch, but the students remained. The librarian got scared, so she called the police.

Soon ten or eleven police arrived, outnumbering the students. Some wore uniforms and some dressed in plain clothes. An officer approached Al Lassiter who stood out at six feet six inches tall.

The policeman barked, "Boy, what are you doing in the library?"

The young man responded politely, "Sir, we want to check out books."

"Your library is down on Mill Street."

Lassiter politely informed him, "Yes, sir. They don't have the books that we need."

The officer commanded: "But you've got to go down there anyway."

Eventually, the chief of detectives, M. B. Pierce, announced, "You all will have to leave."

The students sat silently.

Pierce informed them, "The Colored library is on Mill Street; you all will have to leave."

Still no movement.

"All right, you are under arrest," Pierce announced, "now move out."

At that command, the students got up and allowed the police

The Tougaloo Nine exiting the Jackson Public Library as they are being arrested.

Jackson police mugshots of four of the Tougaloo Nine: clockwise from top left, Alfred Cook, Geraldine Edwards, Joseph Jackson Jr., and Ethel Sawyer.

to lead them out. They passed by that menacing White mob Ethel Sawyer had seen outside the window and got into the waiting police cars. They had been in the library for only ten minutes. The police drove them down to the station, took mug shots of each, and then placed them in four cells, separating the young men and women.

IN JAIL

Geraldine Hollis remembered the cell as the "most horrible, stinky, place I have ever encountered." Several of the nine reported that the food was pretty bad.

They had thought they'd get bail and be out quickly, but officials told them that the person who arranged bail was not around that day. So they stayed in their cells for thirty-six hours without contact from the outside.

To pass the time, Hollis, studying to become a physical education teacher, danced in her cell.

When he heard they would not be released quickly, Joseph Jackson, remembering Emmett Till and so many other lynchings, became afraid: "I was in fear of my life."

During those thirty-six hours, police took the students from their cells and questioned each one. Hollis recalled that the police placed her in a room the size of a broom closet. A man had his foot on her chair as he asked three times, "You know you're not smart enough to plan something like that. Didn't Medgar Evers really plan this?" The police couldn't believe that a group of Black college students staged such an event and they wanted desperately to get something on Evers.

Though the police never allowed the students to see what the community sent, many people stepped up to offer support, sending food, kind notes, and offers of personal property to put up for bond. On Tuesday, March 28, 1961, the day after the read-in and the day before the trial, the community held a mass rally at the College Hill Baptist Church in support of the Tougaloo Nine. Eight hundred people attended.

Support also soon came from fellow college students across town.

The Ladner Sisters Respond

Not far from downtown Jackson where the Nine sat in jail, some students at Jackson State College, including the Ladner sisters, feeling solidarity with their Tougaloo comrades, decided to make a statement. At five o'clock Dorie and Joyce roamed the college cafeteria to invite students to meet in front of the college library for a seven o'clock prayer vigil. Joyce hoped fifty students would attend. Seven hundred showed up.

As those who had gathered prayed for their fellows in jail, Jackson State President Jacob Reddix arrived, accompanied by local police.

According to Joyce Ladner, Reddix "came running through the crowd screaming, hollering 'What is going on, what is going on.' . . . And he went berserk because no one would listen to him. He went from one person to another pushing people." He came up to Joyce and her roommate, shoving Joyce's roommate to the ground and ordering students to go back to the dormitory. Only after Reddix threatened expulsion did students return to their rooms.

But the Ladners had just started.

The next day when the Tougaloo Nine had their court date, students from Jackson boycotted their classes and held a rally attended by two hundred; then fifty marched to the city jail where the Nine were being held. They had not gone far when they encountered a line of Jackson city police with two German shepherd police dogs. As Joyce describes it, ". . . we attempted to stage a demonstration to march down to the courthouse. We were stopped several blocks from the campus. Police had tear gas, billy clubs, and police dogs." The *New York Times* reported, "When the students refused to disband the police started swinging clubs." Joyce shared, "My sister still has scars on her back from the tear gas pellets and her hair fell out for years." When the march broke up as the students fled, the police sicced the dogs on the fleeing students.

Terrified, Joyce ran down an alley and started knocking on a door crying, "Please help, help, they are trying to kill us. Let me in." A "nice lady," a local supporter, offered refuge to her and to others. Other students hid in the local Black-owned funeral parlor. Then, students slowly straggled back to campus.

Next day President Reddix shut the entire campus down early for the Easter holiday. When the Ladners returned from break, they had to meet with the dean of students to discuss their expulsion, but Dorie and Joyce informed the dean that expulsion was not necessary. Next fall they would be transferring to Tougaloo College.

THE TRIAL OF THE TOUGALOO NINE

The trial for the Nine took place on Wednesday, March 29. Across the street from the courthouse, around a hundred supporters of the Tougaloo Nine waited. They were not allowed inside. When the nine students marched up the courthouse steps, the crowd cheered in support. That expression of sympathy incensed the police who attacked the crowd with dogs and swinging clubs. Medgar Evers, who was in that crowd, described the scene: "Instantly, there was a call from police officers saying 'get 'em out of here' and it was then that hordes of policemen and two vicious police dogs converged on Negro citizens only; and began whipping us with night sticks as well as extending the leashes on the dog to the extent that Reverend S. Leon Whitney, pastor of Farish Street Baptist Church, was bitten on the arm. . . . [I] was struck a number of times in the back by officers with billy clubs, and on the head with a pistol, by a man in plainclothes."

Inside the courtroom, the Nine pleaded "not guilty" to a charge of breach of the peace. Though they all pleaded "not guilty," one of the young women later admitted that she had thought, "If I disturbed your peace when I went to the library, then I'm guilty!"

The Judge asked Police Chief W. D. Rayfield, "What were these people doing in the library that constituted a breach of the peace?"

The chief responded: "They were sitting around and reading. But the resentment of the people around the library could have caused a breach of the peace."

Rayfield later told a reporter, "We were getting along very nicely until these people came with the intent to create trouble. They were the source of the trouble and I believed we should remove the source."

Many Whites, including officials, thought the Black community liked the Jim Crow world and only rebelled against it when outsiders came in and put ideas in their heads, ignoring the fact that most of the people protesting lived in Mississippi.

The city court convicted the nine students, fined them one hundred dollars each, and sentenced them to thirty-day suspended jail sentences.

That night, the community gathered for a mass meeting. Despite the presence of police, "tornado warnings and torrential downpours," fifteen hundred attended and celebrated the Tougaloo Nine. As Hollis said, "We had the emotional support and love of which we were very appreciative."

After their lawyers appealed the convictions, all sentences were overturned.

THE IMPORTANCE OF THE TOUGALOO NINE

In a letter to Roy Wilkins of the NAACP, Medgar Evers said, "These young people exhibited the greatest amount of courage in the face of mounting tension and were reported in our local newspapers as being 'orderly, intelligent, and cooperative' . . . This act of bravery on the part of these nine young people has seemed to electrify Negroes' desire for freedom here in Mississippi, . . ." Myrlie Evers went even further stating, "The change of tide in Mississippi . . . began . . . when nine Negro students from Tougaloo Southern Christian College . . . entered Jackson's White public library, sat down, and began to read."

In many respects, the actions of the Tougaloo Nine seemed straightforward—no big deal. Often, it is those seemingly small actions, thought about in deep ways, that make the biggest difference. And so much followed from the simple actions of the Tougaloo Nine.

3   The 'Children' of Medgar Evers

AMOS BROWN GETS ACTIVE IN JACKSON

Emmett Till's murder traumatized Amos Brown too. As he said, "I remember very vividly when Emmett Till's body was discovered on August 28, 1955. I picked up that *Jet* magazine and saw this grotesque, mutilated, horrifying image of a human being. That terrorized me as a child." In 1955 Brown had turned fourteen, the same age as Emmett.

And just months before in nearby Belzoni, Mississippi, a gunman murdered the Reverend George Lee, an activist minister who fought for the right to vote.

Lee had received a threatening note warning him to remove his name from the voting rolls. Soon after the warning, one Saturday evening, Lee drove into town to pick up his suit from the cleaners, something one could do late at night in a small community. As Lee drove home at midnight, a car pulled alongside and someone in the car fired several shots at the minister, hitting him in the jaw. His car crashed into a nearby house. Before a taxi could get him to the hospital, he died.

Typically, the local sheriff did little to investigate the murder, at first calling the event just a traffic accident and later saying that Lee had been killed by "some jealous nigger," adding, "He was quite a ladies' man." As the new field secretary for the NAACP, Medgar Evers investigated Lee's murder. Despite Evers's work and the involvement of the FBI, no one was ever prosecuted for the crime.

Brown knew about the murder and how justice had not been served. His father, also a minister, took Lee's place at the pulpit.

Brown recognized a pattern. Black lives mattered little outside the African American community. As he said, "It was commonplace for me to hear of the tales of lynchings, of Blacks being mysteriously unaccounted for in the Mississippi Delta." Growing up Black in Jackson during the 1940s and '50s, Amos could place this pattern of murders into a broader system: ". . . I was born in a segregated, apartheid South in Mississippi, when things were really difficult."

AMOS BROWN SPEAKS OUT

Brown realized that he needed to do more than just rage about these conditions; he knew that he had to act as well. Inspired by his sister who was already active in the NAACP, Brown organized the first local NAACP youth council in Jackson. Eventually, in the spring of 1956 at the age of fifteen, he became president of the West Jackson Youth Council.

Work with the NAACP connected him with Medgar Evers who became a "surrogate father," Brown recalled. "Mr. Evers was a very humble, warm, engaging man. And he discovered my interests, my talents, and my abilities, even as a lad. He encouraged me."

Brown traveled with Evers throughout the Delta, attending mass meetings and investigating problems that people in the Jim Crow South faced. Evers also took Amos to several NAACP conventions. In 1956 at a convention in San Francisco, they visited the church that Brown would one day lead as minister. Evers also brought him to a convention in Cleveland, a trip that led to trouble.

It was 1958, the summer before Brown's senior year. At the convention Brown talked to a reporter from the *Cleveland Plain Dealer* about the atrocious state of Black schools in Mississippi.

In the article that followed, Brown explained how segregated Black schools received less funds than their White counterparts, resulting in inferior conditions for the Black schools. He told the reporter about his own school where "one night the ceiling from the biology room caved in." He built his case further, explaining, ". . . that we had to read from used textbooks, if we played in the band, we got used instruments, young ladies who studied home economics had to work on used stoves, everything second class." Brown also pointed out that Black teachers in Mississippi got paid far less than their White counterparts, and he wrapped his argument up with "there's nothing equal about educational opportunities for Blacks in Mississippi."

When Brown returned to Jackson, Luther Marshall, his principal, called him and his mother to the school office. When Marshall pulled out a device to record their conversation, Brown knew he was in trouble.

The principal informed Amos that he would not be permitted to reenroll at Jim Hill High School for his senior year because Brown showed disrespect for the administration and was a bad influence on the other students. As the conversation continued, it became clear that Marshall was angry over the comments Brown made to the Cleveland reporter. Reading between the lines, Brown translated the reason for his expulsion: "I didn't know how to keep my mouth shut and I was creating too much trouble." Apparently, both the White and Black school superintendents had ordered Marshall to expel Brown.

Evers got wind of what Marshall had done, and he and other NAACP representatives paid the principal a visit, demanding that Brown be readmitted and threatening to file a lawsuit to integrate the local White high school. The administrators backed off. They allowed Brown to finish his senior year at Jim Hill, but those same powers chose to make things difficult for him in other ways.

Brown was elected president of the student council, but Marshall abolished it. He won the election for senior class president, but the administrators withheld his right to hold the office. When Brown earned the rank of class valedictorian, Marshall knocked him down to salutatorian.

None of this stopped Amos Brown.

SITTING DOWN AT THE ZOO

Upon his high school graduation in 1959, Brown attended Morehouse College in Atlanta, taking a course with Dr. Martin Luther King Jr., the only course Dr. King ever taught. At Morehouse Brown continued his activism, joining sit-ins in Atlanta and leading a wade-in along the Gulf Coast to integrate beaches.

Back home in Jackson for the summer, Amos and some friends decided to fight segregation at the Jackson Zoo. Black people could go to the zoo as long as they didn't sit down to rest: "You couldn't sit on the same bench and look at the monkeys or the elephants together with Whites." How weird is that?

So Brown and some friends tested these restrictions. They went to the zoo, but when Brown got tired, he sat down on the bench where his friends soon joined him. An hour later, police arrived and told them to get up, but they just sat there. So the police arrested them. At the trial, Brown and his co-conspirators were convicted and placed on one-year probation.

The city attorney who tried the case "reasonably" explained why the no-sitting rule existed: ". . . we know from long practice of mixing of the races here in Jackson, places where they stand up together friction does not occur. But there tends to be friction if they sit down together." Then Jackson Mayor Allen Thompson solved the zoo's bench problem once and for all: he removed the benches so nobody could sit.

Amos Brown went on to become a minister and to earn a doctorate. He has remained an activist his entire life, serving since 1976 as pastor of San Francisco's Third Baptist Church—the church he first visited as a young man with Medgar Evers in 1956. This large urban church continues the legacy that Evers inspired when he took a young Brown under his wing. An integral part of an active community, Third Baptist partners with people from all walks of life and faiths as a church committed to "civic engagement and social action, . . . [and] involved in the political processes that affect the plight of underprivileged minority communities." Evers would be proud!

Johnny Frazier Shakes up Greenville

"I had a sense of what was not right and wanted to do something about it." So said Johnny Frazier about his hometown, Greenville, Mississippi. As a teen, he became active in the local fight for civil rights. In 1957 Frazier started a youth chapter of the NAACP, a chapter that grew to fifty or sixty members. "We would have meetings to discuss what was going on, to raise our consciousness." He was around fifteen at the time.

As a young man, Frazier often stood up alone. For instance, on Sunday, March 7, 1960, he attended a local White Episcopalian Church, sitting in the back during the morning service. Like everything else in Greenville, churches were segregated. According to one report, "he was the only Negro present." When the minister asked him why he had come, Frazier explained "he heard over the radio the public was invited."

Two months later, Frazier and two others got kicked out of high school. Their offense? Wearing black armbands to their segregated Black high school, and carrying placards that read, "Remember the Supreme Court Decision." This was six years after the 1954 *Brown v. Board* decision that called for an end to segregated schools.

The principal called the three to the office and ordered them to remove the armbands. Frazier refused, stating years later, "I thought what [the *Brown* decision] represented and symbolized was greater than complying with the rule that the principal laid down, so I chose to be expelled. And I was expelled."

The expulsion brought Medgar Evers, Frazier's mentor, to town.

First Evers spoke at the evening mass rally called to support the three expelled students. The next day he conferred with the school principal and demanded that the students be readmitted. If they weren't, he threatened to petition to have them sent to the local all-White school, an act that would have created more uproar. The principal allowed the three students back into school.

This was the start of a relationship that became very close. Evers's role as state chair of the NAACP and Frazier's leadership in the Greenville NAACP youth council brought them together. Frazier recalled years later, "He kept me under his wing. He was there for me during my difficult times when I was confused. He was there for me in all sorts of ways. . . . He had me at his house. I was like one of his kids."

Still a high school student, Frazier next went after a degrading practice that irked him.

At Sam Stein's, a local department store, Blacks could not use the changing room to try on clothes. They had to measure themselves at home, go to the store, estimate whether or not an item of clothing would fit, and then purchase it. But if the item didn't fit, they couldn't return it or exchange it because White shoppers would not purchase items that had been tried on by Blacks.

In his role as head of the NAACP youth council, Frazier approached the store owner and asked him to change this demeaning policy, but "he declined my request. And of course I put together some kids and we picketed his store." Frazier organized a boycott of the store, Black patrons stopped shopping there, and eventually the store owner gave in and changed the repugnant practice.

Next Frazier and his NAACP youth council fought to have the city hire more Black police. There was only one. When Frazier's appeal to the chief of police was turned down, "I picketed the police station and I was promptly arrested."

This particular protest did not succeed, but others did! For instance, the youth council picketed other stores to push them to hire more Black clerks—lo and behold, stores complied!

PUSHBACK

Despite these promising outcomes, something disturbing happened to Frazier in August of 1960, a year when he was eighteen. Returning from a national youth council meeting in Atlanta, he decided to ride in the front of the bus, an act that violated custom, though not law.

Frazier's behavior so angered the driver that he stopped in Winona, Mississippi, to inform law enforcement officers of Frazier's "violations," and police arrested Frazier for disturbing the peace. The sheriff, Earl Wayne Patridge, alleged that Frazier had used "abusive language" in the Winona terminal.

Frazier tells a different version. When the bus arrived in Winona, Sheriff Patridge got on the bus and told him, "Nigger, you need to go back to the back, because you know that's where you belong!" Frazier refused. When he was taken to jail, ". . . I was brutally beaten where my face was swollen. My body was swollen." The police then poured whiskey into his wounds so they would hurt worse.

The sheriff made the whole experience hell for Frazier. He took the mattress off the bed and left only the metal grate. In the evening he blasted the air conditioning to freeze Frazier, but during the day he turned the air conditioning off and the bed grates became so hot Frazier could not sit on the bed.

And then on the second night, the sheriff allowed a group of people from the town to come in and continue the beating and torture. Frazier's condition was so bad, a doctor eventually had to be called in.

After three days without being allowed a phone call, authorities finally permitted Frazier to call his uncle, who then contacted Medgar Evers. Evers appeared first thing Monday, and eventually Frazier was let out of jail. He was tried and convicted and fined fifty dollars.

Throughout the course of his work with the NAACP youth council from 1958–1963, the Mississippi Sovereignty Commission, a state agency established in 1956 to spy on people involved in the civil rights movement, continuously harassed Frazier, filing more than one hundred reports on his activities. One report warned that Frazier, "a young Negro male about nineteen years of age was perhaps Greenville's most future trouble maker."

FRAZIER AND HIS MENTOR

After high school, Frazier went to college in Jackson, Mississippi, first attending Campbell College and then Tougaloo College. He continued his work with the NAACP youth council and Evers, even applying to the University of Southern Mississippi (USM), hoping to integrate this school that excluded Blacks. Though the school rejected Frazier, two Black students were admitted in 1965.

Years later Frazier, remembering his exclusion from USM, said, "You don't have to stop at the point where you are rejected. . . . In the midst of insanity, you confront it, you make it humorous, you laugh at it. . . . You do not allow it to define who you are, what you are, or what your potential is." After his rejection from USM, Frazier graduated from Tougaloo and later attended Tufts, Harvard, and England's Oxford University, and went on to become a Unitarian minister, living first in Cleveland and later in North Carolina.

The more Frazier worked in the Mississippi movement, the more his relationship with Evers deepened. Years later he stated,

I recall mostly and I can see it right now as if he was right here. I recall Medgar's warm smile, his intensity about Black folks and the condition of Black folks, his passion. I recall his anger. He had an incredible will and determination. . . . He was just a very special passionate person. A wonderful man. Absolutely wonderful man.

Everyone, but especially the young, needs mentors. Medgar Evers was a model for such mentoring, then and still today.

Elders II—The Education of Bob Moses

A Young Man in Harlem

Bob Moses roamed Harlem with his dad, a "man of the street." Young Robert loved hearing that adult conversation, including the back and forth about events in the world. Later he would take in his dad's critique of what people had said. Moses came down particularly hard on the people he called "educated fools," those folks who had college degrees and other credentials but no common sense.

Those critiques call to mind a later encounter with one of Bob's professors at Harvard who thought himself kind for not calling on Bob, his one Black student. Figuring all Blacks to be intellectually inferior and likely to sound stupid in an exalted Harvard classroom, the professor did not want to embarrass Moses. Would this teacher fit that "educated fool" category, given the intellectual gifts of Robert Parris Moses?

Born in 1935, Bob grew up in Harlem and lived in the Harlem River Houses, a public housing project built for working-class African Americans. His dad worked as a janitor at a nearby armory, bitter that he did not have the educational opportunities he knew would have served him well and suited his depth of intelligence.

Robert, on the other hand, did receive that education. He attended a high school for the gifted and then Hamilton College, a small liberal arts institution in upstate New York. One of Moses's classmates described Hamilton at that time as "a largely racist, sexist, anti-Semitic collection of White males," and another classmate acknowledged a distance between Moses and the other students, explaining that ". . . so many of us had never really related to Blacks in any significant way before. He lived . . . in some isolation. . . . Yet he was deeply, widely . . . universally respected."

Moses later told an interviewer that in his high school days he felt frustrated because ". . . you had to be treated as a Negro and you couldn't really be accepted as an individual . . . at any level of the society you happened to penetrate."

After Hamilton, Moses became a graduate student at Harvard, studying analytical philosophy and mathematical logic. After his mother died, he left Harvard to take care of his ailing father, leaving with a master's degree. He then taught math for several years at Horace Mann School, a private college-preparatory high school.

In 1960 something on TV caught Moses's attention and changed him forever: four students from North Carolina A&T College in Greensboro, North Carolina, were sitting-in to protest segregation. "They were kids my age, and I knew this had something to do with my own life."

Those four Black students sitting at a Woolworth's lunch counter sparked a movement. As more students throughout the country joined sit-ins, Moses noted, "I was mesmerized by the pictures I saw almost every day on the front page of the *New York Times*—young committed Black faces seated at lunch counters or picketing, directly and with great dignity, challenging white supremacy in the South. They looked like I felt."

Those images of protest guided Bob Moses toward his calling. After participating in some demonstrations in Newport News, Virginia, and working with activist Bayard Rustin in Harlem, Moses traveled to Atlanta, Georgia, where, at twenty-five, he began his life's work as a full-time civil rights activist.

BOB MOSES COMES TO MISSISSIPPI

Heading south, ready to learn all he needed to foment a revolution, Moses was lucky to study with the masters.

In the summer of 1960, he ended up in the Atlanta office of the Southern Christian Leadership Conference (SCLC), the organization Dr. King cofounded after the Montgomery Bus Boycott. Moses quickly gravitated to the Student Nonviolent Coordinating Committee —SNCC (pronounced "snick")—a natural home for him given that SNCC had emerged from the student sit-ins that had started him on this path.

In the small SNCC office, he met the great Ella Baker, a powerful and important movement leader who had helped to shape SCLC and to start SNCC. Like Medgar Evers and other elders, she also mentored many young people finding their way into the movement.

Baker became a guide and a teacher for Moses: "She asked me about my upbringing, my thoughts on Harlem, my entrance into the movement. Her interest in me was what struck me; . . . Mrs. Baker was actually talking to me." Through her questioning, Baker was demonstrating her theory of how to organize people.

As a fieldworker for the NAACP during the thirties and forties, Baker had traveled throughout the South and built the organization one person at a time, just as Evers had. That was her strategy for organizing: connect with the ordinary people. Everywhere Baker went, she took the time to get to know the folks she met, helping them to see themselves as leaders and as individuals who could change their own world, teaching them "that they cannot look for salvation anywhere but themselves." Bob Moses absorbed these essential ideas.

So in 1960 when SNCC's members wanted to link with activists in the deep South, Moses volunteered. Guided by Baker's spirit and experience, he got on a bus and rode to Alabama and then Mississippi, the most racially troubled states in America.

Baker gave him a list of contacts, people who had been fighting for civil rights for years. The list included Amzie Moore in Cleveland, Mississippi. Like Evers, Moore had been active in the struggle since returning from fighting overseas during World War II. He headed the local NAACP and was vice-president of the state chapter.

When Moses arrived in Cleveland, it seemed as if Moore had been waiting for him. They hit it off immediately. "As we traveled, Amzie schooled me, giving me a detailed oral history of the state, explaining motives and politics . . . and possibilities." The two talked on and on. As Moses said, "Ideas simply didn't intimidate him and I found conversation with him invigorating and liberating."

Moses spent much of that summer with Moore, staying at his house, traveling around the community, meeting people, and learning. This experience must have felt like those days when the

Bob Moses thinking and working in what is likely the Jackson voter-registration office.

young Moses walked the streets of Harlem with his dad. In fact, Moses called Moore "my father in the movement."

Moore challenged Moses early by having him talk to church groups where Moses would tell the people, "There's something coming. Get ready. It's inevitably coming your way whether you like it or not."

Later Moses proudly reported, "I must have passed Amzie's tests because he encouraged me to work with him." Moore wanted SNCC to send young people like Moses to Mississippi. He foresaw that the young people would start the campaign, and the community would then pick up the fight.

Moses was on board. All he needed to do was fulfill his teaching contract at Horace Mann School. So in the summer of 1961, after the school year ended, Moses returned to Cleveland and his work with Moore.

Then in July, C. C. Bryant, president of the Pike County, Mississippi, NAACP chapter, asked Moore for a SNCC team to come to McComb in the southwest part of the state to start a campaign. So Moore sent Moses. At the start, Moses was the team. Little did he know the dangers he would face or the powerful movement he would help to create.

4 Brenda Travis and the Burglund High Walkout

BRENDA TRAVIS IS BORN AND GROWS UP

Within the embrace of family and the warmth of community, Brenda Travis lived a childhood filled with love. But once she stepped beyond the protection of kin and neighbor, she swam in a sea of animosity that had affected her even before her birth.

Her parents worked as sharecroppers in the Mississippi Delta, eking out a deplorable existence raising cotton, working from sunup to sundown but always trapped in poverty. The plantation her parents, Icie Martin and LS Travis, lived on was owned by a man named Moon Mullin.

In March of 1945, Mullin ordered Mrs. Travis out into the field to work the cotton; she was nine months pregnant with Brenda at the time. Mr. Travis protested that his wife was about to deliver a baby. The enraged Mullin went to get his gun. Travis ran home to his wife, telling her, "Don't pack anything. Just get the bare necessities. We've got to go." The Travises fled south to McComb, Mississippi, home of Mrs. Travis's parents, where Brenda was safely born. Fearing for his life if he stayed, Brenda's dad took off. Today she believes that "my activism in the civil rights movement was always predetermined, even from the womb."

Brenda Travis grew up in McComb surrounded by the love of her mom, her grandmother, and her brothers and sisters. It was a life of poverty, but it was a good life, mainly because of the warmth of family and community, but also in part because it included little interaction with Whites. The contact that did occur between the races was often negative. Travis remembers that outside her own community, "McComb was a hotbed of hatred, discrimination, racism."

Travis learned early that the hatred extended beyond McComb. While she was still growing up, Emmett Till was murdered, and she felt that brutal killing deeply. She still remembers her reaction as a ten-year-old to the picture of Emmett's body: "Then the *Jet* magazine came out and it showed this person that was battered and beaten beyond recognition." The picture left her traumatized.

She wondered what Emmett Till could possibly have done to warrant such savagery. Though the murder was meant to scare Blacks, for Brenda Travis, "it took the opposite effect. . . . It was my motivation to say 'One day. One Day.'"

Emmett's murder took on a real presence for young Travis. Around the same time, the sheriff came demanding to know the whereabouts of her thirteen-year-old brother, James. When her grandmother asked why he wanted to know, the sheriff responded, "Shut up, old lady!" And when she asked what he was accused of doing, he again ordered her to "Shut up!" As Travis relates, "I recall the sheriff coming there like the Gestapo, there was no knock, I mean, he just bust the door open, blast the door open. And my brother was still in bed, and they snatched him up from the bed." Travis was terrified. As she told a group of interviewers, when the sheriff took her brother away, "the only thing I could envision was that he was going to end up like Emmett Till."

The authorities released James after a brief jail stay, offering no apology and providing no explanation for why he had been held. Facing that cruelty, at that moment Travis's strongest feeling was relief: "I thought he would die. When I saw him again I held him with everything I had. I never wanted to let him go."

Later Travis's relief gave way to anger, and she swore she would act when the time came: "I was sick and tired of being treated like a second-class . . . well I won't even call it second-class citizen. A noncitizen. Like not even being born in America."

As Travis grew up, she gravitated toward action, especially once she saw that others shared her thinking, others who had had enough. One night she heard an older man, C. C. Bryant, the president of McComb's NAACP, speak at church. At that moment, Travis knew she was not alone.

Then came the final push. Still a young teen, Travis had been working in a laundry from the time she was twelve. One day her boss, dissatisfied with how a shirt had been ironed, threatened Travis physically. Tired of disrespect and humiliation, she acted. According to her account, "I put the iron down. I collected my little sandwich, and I left out. And I went directly to Bryant to join the NAACP. Coincidentally, that was the day that Bob Moses appeared in McComb looking to solicit people to help with voter registration." Meeting Moses, Travis became one more young person who joined the movement.

DIRECT ACTION: HOLLIS WATKINS AND CURTIS HAYES

Hollis Watkins, another Mississippi teen, had also thought long and hard about the freedom struggle. So he attended meetings of the local NAACP youth council where he encountered Medgar Evers. Watkins recalled, "At those meetings Medgar was really trying to encourage and promote young people to get involved and to take out membership in the NAACP and . . . to get Black people registered to vote."

After high school, Watkins headed to California where he could live with his sister and look for work. But one night, while watching television, Watkins saw images of Freedom Riders from back home in Mississippi. Those images became a call, and he returned home to join the movement.

During the summer of 1961, Watkins, Curtis Hayes (today, Curtis Muhammad) and two other friends heard the rumor that Martin Luther King Jr. had come to McComb! Eager to meet Dr. King, they headed to the Masonic Temple where they discovered Bob Moses instead.

On first impression, Moses did not appear to be much like the dynamic King. Watkins acknowledged, "Well, he seemed just like a normal, shy, you know, quiet, . . . serious man." But despite that quiet manner, Moses possessed his own charisma and a gentle, thoughtful nature that drew others to him and earned their respect and loyalty. Moses talked to the four young men about voter registration and invited Watkins to go through the registration process so he could teach the process to others. Watkins complied.

Moses taught Watkins and Hayes, his first local recruits, the Ella Baker style of organizing: Go door-to-door and get to know the people!

Soon the two headed out into McComb and leafleted the community. According to Watkins, ". . . we instantly began to hit the streets and asked people to come out to the voter registration meetings, come out to the mass meetings, and then encouraged them to go on down to the courthouse and register to vote."

To expand movement activity, Moses brought SNCC to McComb. SNCC set up headquarters in the Masonic Temple, "a two-story combination cinder block and paintless wood structure which housed a grocery store on the street level and a Masonic meeting hall above it."

Watkins and Hayes soon became involved in all aspects of SNCC activity. Then, in late August of 1961, Marion Barry came to McComb to form the Pike County Nonviolent Direct Action

Committee, the part of SNCC that leaned more toward the confrontational sit-ins and marches and away from the slower door-to-door organizing.

Meeting Barry, Watkins and Hayes wanted to try the direct action approach.

Knowing the situation in McComb, the two figured they would start by integrating the local library. So they soon headed over to the McComb Library where Blacks were forbidden, but they found the staff had hung a sign: "We are closed today."

So next they marched over to the local Woolworth's department store to sit-in at the Whites-only lunch counter. Every seat was taken, but they waited until a woman and her child left and quickly sat down. Watkins described what happened next: "The waitress went to the other end of the counter and, by that time, the police were there asking us to move or else we would be arrested. They said it three times and finally said, 'You're arrested,' and walked us down to the city hall." Arrested for "breach of peace," Watkins and Hayes were convicted and spent thirty-four days in jail.

The night of the pair's arrest, SNCC held a mass meeting in the Masonic Temple. Rather than the ten to fifteen who usually attended such meetings, two hundred from the community showed up, numbers that validated the power of the direct action approach. Leaders asked for volunteers to join the sit-ins to sustain the momentum started by the two young men. Brenda Travis, sitting in the audience that night, quickly volunteered.

A Word about Nonviolence

When Watkins and Hayes sat in, like students in Nashville and Greensboro, North Carolina, they were using tactics borrowed from advocates of nonviolence. You'll be hearing more about this philosophy, so here is a quick explanation.

The terms nonviolent and nonviolence are an important part

of the civil rights movement. Martin Luther King Jr., for instance, was a proponent of the philosophy and tactic of nonviolence. The students who formed SNCC also initially proclaimed nonviolence as central to their credo.

The philosophy of nonviolence that Americans used primarily grew out of ideas developed by Mahatma Mohandas Gandhi, the Indian activist and spiritual leader, who lived from 1869–1948. Gandhi developed and employed his theory of nonviolence to encourage the British to end their rule over India. It worked.

U.S. activists listened carefully to Gandhi, but they also honed their beliefs about nonviolence with other sources that included the New Testament and the thinking of Henry David Thoreau.

Nonviolence used during the days of the civil rights movement meant that activists would not retaliate when struck. The goal was to transform so-called enemies, encouraging them to see activists and demonstrators as human beings. As proponents of nonviolence said, the goal is not to defeat adversaries but to change them. As an additional benefit, the photographs and videos of those quiet, dignified protestors attempting to eat in public places or to exercise their rights to peacefully march—while being met with heavily armed White men, attacked by police dogs, and beaten and humiliated by hate-filled mobs—showed the rest of America the circumstances under which Black citizens in the South lived.

It requires great discipline for those struck to not strike back. Activists in the civil rights movement studied nonviolent philosophy and trained themselves for what they would face. Not everyone in the movement was committed to nonviolence. Some followed it only as a tactic without buying into the whole philosophy. Others carried guns and advocated self-defense. In fact, nonviolence as a means to gain civil rights was actively debated by people in the movement. And SNCC, an organization that started with a clear endorsement of the philosophy and practice of nonviolence, saw

some of its members move away from that endorsement, to different degrees, as the years went on.

BRENDA TRAVIS GETS ARRESTED

By the age of sixteen, Travis had become an activist, first with
the NAACP and then with SNCC. Bob Moses described her as a
"young girl" who "had been very active with us in voter registration
in McComb. And I mean active. She had walked the streets every
day with us . . . in the hot sun."

Though she had worked hard going door-to-door, she grew
frustrated. Sometimes when some people saw her coming, they
ran into the house, afraid to go to the courthouse and suffer the
retribution from Whites that would inevitably follow. Who could
blame them? Voting registrars treated Blacks rudely, generally
denying them the right to vote for silly reasons—they signed their
names on the wrong line of the application or they did not know
how many bubbles were contained in a bar of soap, a ludicrous
question Whites sometimes asked Blacks as part of the voting test.
Some people who attempted to register lost their jobs, and there
was always the lingering fear of nightriders. So while avoiding
community organizers like the plague made some sense, for Travis,
"That was difficult to accept."

Travis felt ready to engage in the direct action approach Marion
Barry had brought to McComb. She and just a few other volunteers
trained with Barry, learning how to respond nonviolently to any
violent behavior they might face. So when the chance for direct
action appeared, Travis was ready! The night before her first sit-in,
she prayed, asking God to protect her and her family while thinking, "I knew I was going to jail."

The next day, Travis and two comrades, Ike Lewis and Robert
Talbot, needed determination. They went first to the train station
to integrate the Whites-only lunch counter, but found the door

locked. Next they went up the street to the Woolworth's, but the waitresses filled up all seats at the lunch counter. The third attempt proved the charm.

Travis, Lewis, and Talbot marched from the Masonic Temple over to the Greyhound bus station and walked in, surprising the White customers as the three headed straight for the White waiting room to purchase tickets. Quiet first filled the station as hostile stares assaulted the three activists, but when they moved to purchase tickets, angry words, including "nigger," flew, and Travis feared the crowd was getting ready to attack. Ironically, relief came when police arrived and arrested the three.

Travis spent that night in jail and then twenty-eight more days, sleeping during the day and, to keep her spirits up, praying and singing at night. Her mother visited as often as she could, despite having no car and the jail being eight miles down the road from McComb. Years later, in discussing the bus station protest, Travis explained, "To be honest, I was really excited because there wasn't much going on in McComb . . . so this was sort of like the highlight of our being, the highlight of our existence . . ."

All her life Travis had been taught to dread jail, but once inside a jail for the first time in her life she found that being in jail for standing up and fighting for justice gave her a sense of peace.

THE BURGLUND HIGH SCHOOL WALKOUT

After she finally got out of jail that October, Travis returned to Burglund High School, ready to start the school year, but that year never happened. Commodore Dewey Higgins, the principal, did not permit her to return. When she asked why, Higgins said he had no choice, that the White school superintendent had ordered him to expel her. It angered Travis that a Black principal would let a White administrator bully him, and she let him know it in no uncertain terms: "You mean to tell me you're going to let that

White man tell you what to do with a Colored student?" To which Higgins responded, "I'm doing my job."

Meanwhile, Travis's classmates had heard about Higgins's decision. They were not happy. Jerome Byrd, president of the senior class, organized an informal meeting with other student leaders to discuss the expulsion and how students might respond. Every Wednesday Higgins held a regular school assembly to share upcoming events and to answer student questions. And the assembly was set to occur that day. After thirty minutes, they decided Joe Lewis would interrogate Higgins about Travis publicly.

At the assembly, students heard the usual announcements and the principal's talk, but, finally, it was the students' turn. Higgins invited students to ask any question they wished, but no one spoke. Higgins again solicited questions. Still no response. He asked a third time. Lewis, throwing off a case of nerves, stood up and inquired, "When will Brenda Travis return to school?" The sun was in Higgins's eyes, and he couldn't identify Lewis so he demanded, "Who asked that question?" Lewis did not answer. Higgins then ordered that the student who had asked the question meet with him after the assembly. The student leaders walked to the office with Lewis, not knowing what to do next. They discussed their options quickly and decided to stage a walkout.

At first only some twenty students left the building, so the leaders went back in and walked from classroom to classroom, urging others to join them. The teachers didn't stop the students from coming into classes, but neither did they offer invitations. Seeing the numbers growing, the group went back to classrooms one more time and encouraged their friends to "join the march." Others did. Eventually one hundred and fourteen students walked out. With Travis at the front of the line and everyone singing, "Woke up this morning with my mind on freedom . . . ," they headed to SNCC headquarters, planning to create signs and continue their march.

As the walkout was happening, SNCC members from around the South were meeting at the Masonic Temple, deeply engaged in a strategy session. But the students' singing caught the ears of some at the Temple and disrupted the meeting. As the excited students swarmed in, the slightly older SNCC activists wondered what advice to give to their young comrades to direct their zeal. A discussion between SNCC and the Burglund marchers ensued.

Though everyone in SNCC saw the passion and energy of the marchers, some like Bob Moses discouraged the students, fearing that a march by these teenagers would just anger local racists and accomplish little. Those who favored direct action disagreed. Not wanting to squash the students' enthusiasm, the SNCC members agreed that the march should go on, though Bob Moses discouraged a march to the next county, where Travis had been incarcerated, urging the students to keep the march short and local and suggesting they be orderly by marching in two lines and staying on the sidewalks when possible. The students agreed to take Moses's advice. They grabbed their signs and headed off.

First the young people and some of their SNCC mentors marched down Summit Street, McComb's Black business district. The students' signs proclaimed messages like, "Are you Happy Second Class Citizen?" "A Voteless People is Voiceless, So Vote," and "We Shall Overcome." With placards held high, the students greeted their stunned elders on the street. Heading west on Georgia Street, they sang "We Shall Overcome" and "This Little Light of Mine."

Soon the marchers approached the Illinois Central viaduct, a route which would take them beneath the train tracks. Stomachs tightened. They were heading into White McComb, an area where they knew they were not welcome even under normal circumstances. Young Black kids growing up in McComb had been taught all of their lives those unwritten Jim Crow rules that Emmett Till had not quite learned: not to ride in the front of the bus, not to sit at

Students walking out of Burglund High School in support of
Brenda Travis (right front).

Whites-only lunch counters, and never to play on the White side
of the viaduct.

SNCC member Bob Zellner later remembered the moment:

> As we approached the railroad tracks, things began to get qui-
> eter until you could hear only the shuffle of feet on dusty gravel.
> Even the weather, it seemed, began to change as we crossed from
> "niggertown" to the sidewalks of White McComb. The sky seemed
> darker, and the footfalls were quieter . . .

Soon White residents poked their heads out of shops and
homes. When the marchers got to city hall, a White mob had already formed, with cursing and name-calling in the air. One from
the mob shouted, "You niggers need to go back over to your side
of the track!"

At city hall, Hollis Watkins, who had been at the SNCC meeting and participated in the march, decided to demonstrate a spirit of peace. He climbed to the top of the steps, got down on his knees, and began to pray. Police quickly arrested him. Students followed his example. One by one, the young people mounted the steps, stopping at the top to offer prayers. Police arrested each one. Travis took her turn, ascending the steps and offering prayer, a violation of parole and an invitation to her second arrest.

Meanwhile, the others stood quietly. As the police watched, they must have begun to imagine a long day filled with the arrests, one-by-one, of many praying. So, to get it over with, ". . . the police blew their whistles and pronounced everyone under arrest."

Joe Lewis remembered the rough manner of the police, grabbing the young marchers by the scruff of their necks, demanding meanly, "Boy, what's your name?" and shoving the kids down the stairs toward the jail cells. In the cells, Lewis recalled how, as they looked up through the windows and onto the street, Whites above looked back, dangling nooses and telling the kids, "Nigger, we going to hang you tonight. You will not get out alive! That didn't happen. Police released some students quickly and others in a few days.

Another awful incident occurred in the midst of that pray-in. Seeing Bob Zellner, a White guy, marching with the Black students, the White mob went ballistic, considering Zellner a traitor to his own race. When Zellner took his turn to walk up the steps, members of the mob grabbed and beat him, sticking thumbs in his eyes to tear them out. When Moses came to help, he got pulled away by the crowd. The police just stood by. As Zellner recalled, "They had just every kind of weapon you can imagine: Baseball bats, pipes, wrenches." After the beating, police arrested—not the members of the White mob—but Bob Zellner. He was charged with several crimes, the most severe being contributing to the delinquency of minors. He spent four months in prison.

On October 10, six days later, the students who had marched

returned to Burglund High School and went to their classes. Eventually each got called to the office by Higgins and told that they had to sign a form pledging never to walk out again and acknowledging they would be expelled if they did. Many students decided they would not sign the form and walked out again, marching to the Masonic temple. Ultimately, sixty-four students refused to sign the pledge, all receiving expulsions from their school.

That night the community hosted a mass meeting at the temple. Medgar Evers traveled from Jackson to offer his support.

Fifty of the expelled students then attended an alternative temporary school set up by SNCC, Nonviolent High. Its meetings were first held at the Masonic Temple and later at Campbell College in Jackson. The students studied much of the curriculum they would have encountered at their regular high school, but they also studied one subject not taught at Burglund High, African American history, at that time completely absent from any textbook or curriculum, Black or White. For the first time, the students encountered their own historical world.

Travis was not as fortunate as her classmates. Because her rearrest violated her parole, the judge ordered her to Oakley Training School, a reform school near Raymond, Mississippi. The judge handed out that order without a hearing or trial and without the knowledge of her mother or attorney. And he left the sentence open. Travis did not know how long she would have to stay. Perhaps until she was twenty-one.

It took weeks for Mrs. Travis to find out where her daughter was, and, when she first came to visit, officials did not let her see Brenda, although eventually she was able to.

Travis remained incarcerated for six and a half months. As a condition for her release, the governor ordered her to leave the state of Mississippi. Initially Travis felt broken in many ways by the entire experience, but her views and feelings changed over time.

In 2006, Travis returned for a commemoration of the walkout in McComb, a ceremony that took place at the former Burglund High School (now Higgins Middle School), where she spoke and received a standing ovation. At that commemoration, Travis was able to tell her long-ago comrades, some of whom were present, "I'd like to applaud the students who left this place on my behalf. I haven't really had a chance to thank them." She also encouraged the crowd to continue the fight for justice.

In recalling her arrest and the time she spent in jail, Travis later stated:

Maybe something's wrong with my head, but I was feeling proud, prideful. I had the courage to do it. And many people ask were you afraid. And it was something about the entire experience that I felt no fear. I felt no fear. I guess you could call it much like a vindication. I knew that I was going against the system. I knew I was rebelling against a system that never should have been in place in the first place. So I just felt good. I felt it was doing something positive. And that I was on my journey. I was on the journey that I had vowed to take. That's when my "one day" came.

5   Freedom Riders and
Two Kids from Jackson

· ·

FREEDOM RIDERS IN THE MCCOMB BUS STATION

On November 29, 1961, less than three months after Brenda
Travis's sit-in, five Freedom Riders traveled from New Orleans to
the same Greyhound bus station in McComb and walked into the
same White waiting room. Rather than the surprised White patrons
Travis had met, this time the protestors encountered a violent,
angry mob. Twenty-one year old Jerome Smith, who led the group
of nonviolent Riders, described the scene: "When we entered the
McComb bus station, all these White folks came pouring into the
station shouting, 'Niggers!' and 'Kill 'em!'"

Four Riders sat at the lunch counter while Smith went to the
window and asked to purchase a ticket. The White man at the
ticket window ignored Smith. The White man tending the lunch
counter refused to serve the four Riders, of course. One White
man in the mob picked up a coffee mug and bashed eighteen-year-
old George Raymond in the head, spilling coffee down his back.
Another "jumped" at and punched Smith, then struck him in the
head repeatedly with brass knuckles screaming, "I'll kill him! I'll
kill him! I'll kill him!"

All the Riders, the three men and two women, were punched
or kicked by the Whites and then shoved outside. But, trained in
nonviolence, none of the Riders struck back. Smith and Raymond

were members of the Congress of Racial Equality (CORE), a civil rights organization founded in 1942 and grounded in the Gandhian philosophy of nonviolence.

More Riders followed two days later. A group of six from Baton Rouge strolled into the bus depot and sat for three minutes while a mob of six hundred fumed outside because local police, finally forced by the federal government to follow Interstate Commerce Commission (ICC) mandates, protected the Riders.

Then the following day, a group from Jackson that included three of the expelled Burglund students rode in, spending three minutes in the White waiting room and then going outside to get into a vehicle. A mob attacked the car, but police again protected the Riders.

In truth, the vicious encounters reflected victory for the Freedom Riders and an eventual end to segregation in interstate travel. After five months of Freedom Rides—rides that had been met by beatings, bombings, and massive arrests—the U.S. government finally acted. In a September 22, 1961 ruling, the ICC, the federal agency in charge of laws related to interstate travel, required buses traveling across state lines to display a sign that read, "Seating aboard this vehicle is without regard to race, color, creed, or national origin, by order of the Interstate Commerce Commission." The ICC ordered all terminals used by such buses to stop segregating customers in waiting rooms or at terminal lunch counters. The ruling would go into effect on November 1.

Even the recalcitrant White officials in McComb were forced to abide by the ruling. Signs like the one posted previously by the McComb police chief, signs that said "White Waiting Room—Intrastate Passengers," signs that had moved the Freedom Riders to act and get arrested, had to come down.

That victory took five months of Freedom Riders traveling throughout the South, an action that brought an army of brave, nonviolent activists through Alabama and into Mississippi, peaceful warriors, Black and White, people who came from everywhere in the country. They faced the brutal violence of white supremacists head-on. And then many stayed.

FREEDOM RIDERS

We need to step back a little in time. The Freedom Rides had started in May of 1961, when the first thirteen Riders hit the road (actually, they were not the literal first; a similar ride in 1947 was called the Journey of Reconciliation). The 1961 Riders, male and female, Black and White, separated into two buses, a Greyhound and a Trailways. Their goal: travel as a racially mixed group from Washington, D.C., to New Orleans to force the U.S. government to obey *Boynton v. Virginia*, a 1960 Supreme Court ruling that mandated the integration of interstate public transportation. The ruling meant that separate Black and White waiting rooms in bus stations and Blacks having to sit in the backs of buses had to end. In reality, defying the Supreme Court, segregation in interstate travel continued, and President Kennedy did nothing to stop it.

In response to that inaction, CORE organized the Freedom Rides, hoping to force the ruling into reality just through behavior, with Black Freedom Riders sitting in the fronts of buses and White Riders sitting in the backs, as well as White Riders using the "Colored" bathrooms in depots and Black Riders using "White" facilities.

These simple actions provoked such vicious and violent reactions that the Freedom Rides almost ended in Alabama. When the Greyhound bus stopped at an Anniston, Alabama, terminal on May 14, Whites met the Riders with clubs, pipes, and knives, smashing windows, slashing tires, and terrifying the Riders for twenty minutes before the police arrived. The Whites were members of the Ku Klux Klan (KKK), a violent white supremacist organization that still exists.

The police finally waved the beat-up bus out of the parking lot and into the dangerous Alabama countryside. A parade of Whites in cars and pickups followed. Eight miles out of town, a slashed tire gave out and the bus driver had to stop on the side of the road. Klan members surrounded the bus, rocking it, breaking windows, and calling the Riders to come out and meet their fate. Someone in the mob threw a firebomb into the bus. Klansmen then held the bus door closed to prevent the Riders escaping the toxic smoke and flames. Cries from the mob included "Burn them alive!" and "Fry the goddam niggers!" An undercover state trooper who had been on the bus drew his gun and forced the door open and the mob back to let the Riders off the bus. Some Riders were still beaten. Meanwhile Birmingham civil rights leader Fred Shuttlesworth had been alerted. He quickly organized a convoy of cars which sped to the scene to rescue the Riders and whisk them to Birmingham.

On the same day, the second bus met an equally savage fate. First Klansmen boarded the Trailways bus that had stopped at its Anniston station. They assaulted the Riders, saving the harshest beatings for the two White riders, and then forcing Black Riders to the back of the bus and Whites to the front. Things got worse after the bus traveled the sixty-five miles to the Birmingham Trailways station.

Bull Connor, Birmingham's Commissioner of Public Safety, had close ties to the Klan and let it be known that when the bus got there the police would not be present. Connor granted the KKK members fifteen minutes to do whatever they wanted to the arriving Freedom Riders. The Klansmen used that opportunity maliciously, beating the Riders again, this time inside the terminal. Riders and people merely suspected of being Riders were punched and kicked and bludgeoned. After the allotted fifteen minutes, police arrived, the Klan fled, and local activists saw that the Riders got medical care.

James Peck, a Rider who had been badly beaten, talked to reporters at the hospital where he received fifty-three stitches in his head. When asked if the Ride had been worth it, he responded, "The going is getting rougher, but I'll be on that bus tomorrow headed for Montgomery."

Peck would not get that chance. This group of Freedom Riders felt they had gone as far as possible and ended their Ride by flying the rest of the way to New Orleans.

But as this first group halted their Freedom Ride, a group of college students from Nashville, Tennessee, stepped up. They believed this core principle of nonviolent resistance: violence can not be allowed to stop nonviolent protest. If it does, then violence wins.

These students were also beaten, at the Greyhound station in Montgomery, but their continuation of the Rides eventually forced the Kennedys—President John F. and Attorney General Robert—to protect them as they headed west toward Jackson, Mississippi. There, as part of an agreement with the Kennedys that guaranteed the safety of the Riders as far as Jackson, the police arrested the activists as they stepped into waiting rooms at the Greyhound station. Angered state officials sent many of the Riders to the notorious maximum security Parchman Farm prison in the Mississippi Delta, figuring that the Rides would end if they were tough on the activists.

They were wrong.

With each arrest, more Riders arrived. Throughout the summer of 1961, successive waves of Freedom Riders swept over Mississippi. Four hundred and thirty six Riders participated—women and men, Blacks and Whites, people from all over the country. And thanks to newspaper and TV coverage, the entire nation, the entire world, had witnessed both the courage of the Riders and the violence directed against them just for exercising their civil rights. And the Rides proved to be effective.

The September ICC ruling finally mandated an end to segregation in interstate forms of travel. But just declaring an end didn't necessarily mean segregation *would* end. So activists like Jerome

Freedom Riders being arrested in Jackson in 1961 and taken to the county jail.

Smith and George Raymond pushed to make sure the ruling would be followed. It would take more pressure by activists, serious enforcement efforts by the federal government, and another year and a half before the nation actually ended discrimination once and for all in interstate travel.

But the Rides had even more far-reaching impacts on the Mississippi freedom struggle. For one thing, the Rides brought more activists to Mississippi, some like Diane Nash who organized the rides and others like Joan Trumpauer Mulholland who rode. Many of these organizers and riders remained in Mississippi after serving their time in jail to continue the struggle and energize the Mississippi movement into the future. These Freedom Riders brought a spirit the young people of Mississippi captured for themselves.

LUVAUGHN BROWN: HIS LIFE AS A YOUNG MAN

Luvaughn Brown grew up angry. He never quite knew what to do with the hostility that had been fueled by his abusive father, so Brown brought that anger out onto the streets. "I was always ready to fight," he later recalled. "My answer to everything at that time was violence: You gotta hurt somebody."

Beyond a rough childhood, just growing up in Jackson, Mississippi, during the 1950s and '60s had its ways of infuriating a young Black kid. If the murder of Emmett Till when Brown was eleven wasn't enough, there was the daily insult of segregation. For instance, when he went to the movies, he had to sit in the balcony, the "Colored" section. And, of course, he attended a segregated school, having to walk five miles each way to receive his education. Black kids didn't get school buses.

And, like Johnny Frazier in Greenville, Brown also experienced that degrading practice of shop owners prohibiting Black people from trying on clothes in stores. Brown had to first pay for items, then bring them home to try on. If they didn't fit, his mom would have to rip out and resew the seams so they did. They could not be returned.

And Black children received warnings from their parents about proper behavior in the Jim Crow South, warnings like the ones Emmett Till's mother had tried to give her son. Brown shared,

> Your parents would remind you that you don't disrespect White people. . . . You don't get involved with the cops. You stay where you belong. Because you never knew what was going to happen. People would disappear, end up in the river. You had to be careful. You look at someone the wrong way, and you could be dead. That kind of violence could take place at any time. And that's how I grew up.

LUVAUGHN BROWN BECOMES AN ACTIVIST

In the summer of 1961, the Freedom Riders came to Jackson and their presence changed Brown's life. James Bevel and Bernard Lafayette, two Freedom Riders, went to jail at Parchman Farm and then stayed on in Jackson to organize, helping to form the Jackson Nonviolent Movement. Looking for recruits, they visited local high schools. When they met Brown, they saw the sixteen-year-old as a charismatic and intelligent guy, a potential leader . . . if he could just channel that anger.

Brown liked the two Freedom Riders; he just wasn't sure about the nonviolence stuff that they preached. Still, he recognized that they "really believed in what they were saying."

Finally, after Brown and his friend Jimmie Travis witnessed Bevel and Lafayette's passion one night at an NAACP meeting, the two teens went home and began to devise a scheme to challenge Jim Crow segregation.

Brown and Travis headed over to a downtown Walgreens and walked in, each first buying a toothbrush, then strolling over to the lunch counter where they sat down. A few White people were sitting at the counter, some in nearby booths. Brown and Travis asked to be served, Travis ordering apple pie. The waitress told the two she would not serve them, and the manager told them to leave. They continued to sit.

A crowd began to gather and, as Brown tells it, "The next folks we dealt with were the cops." Jackson police officer L. D. Holliday had arrived. Holliday's arrest report states that he "saw two negroes sitting on the third and fourth stools. I approached these negroes, ordered them to Move On, they just turned their heads, I then told them again to Move On, but they ignored my order at which time I placed them under arrest for Breach of the Peace" [sic].

Brown and Travis spent a brief time in jail before someone bailed them out. The *Clarion-Ledger,* one of Jackson's daily newspapers, reported that "This was the first attempt to integrate downtown Jackson, although 227 'freedom riders' have been jailed here."

Sitting-in was only the beginning. In October, Brown picketed the segregated state fair in Jackson. Police arrested him again.

Later in February of 1962, police hauled Brown and his White movement colleague, Joan Trumpauer, in for questioning. Their crime: they walked into town together, close enough so they could talk. Though the police treated them politely, they warned Trumpauer that she would be arrested for breaking the law if she continued behaving this way. After all, they had caught her and Brown walking together previously. How terrible that Trumpauer, a White girl, walked closely in public with a Black male friend!

Finally, Brown stood up for Diane Nash, an organizer of the Freedom Rides. Nash had been teaching young people the philosophy and practice of nonviolence, so naturally the Jackson police arrested her and charged her with contributing to the delinquency of minors.

At one of Nash's trials, Brown and another friend, Jessie Harris, wanted to show their support. According to SNCC's the *Student Voice*, "Brown and Harris seated themselves on the side of the courtroom reserved for Whites and refused to move when the bailiff ordered them to." They went to jail for contempt and served forty days at Hinds County Prison Farm.

After his difficult youth, Brown found a purpose and a home in the civil rights movement. He eventually joined SNCC, moved to Greenwood, and worked with the legendary Sam Block. Although Brown's civil right activities found him in and out of jail—a criminal life to some—his life has been far different from the one he might have lived had he not channeled that anger. Instead, that jail time marked him as a freedom fighter, one of the "unsung heroes of civil rights."

HEZEKIAH WATKINS GOES TO PARCHMAN FARM

Hezekiah Watkins got arrested as a Freedom Rider at the ripe old age of thirteen. Authorities sent him to the notorious Parchman Farm. An active curiosity, a friend's shove, and a Jim Crow childhood led to his incarceration. An activist life and one hundred arrests followed that first jail experience.

Many years later, Watkins described his childhood in Jackson: "If I wanted water, my place was to drink from the fountain that read 'Colored only.' If I wanted a sandwich, my place was to go to the rear of an establishment. That was my knowledge. That was my belief. That was my understanding of being Black in Jackson, Mississippi, as a thirteen-year-old child."

Then the Freedom Riders came to Jackson during the summer of 1961. Watkins, still in junior high, wanted to learn more, so he attended an NAACP mass meeting at the Masonic Temple. That night he heard a powerful speech delivered by Dr. Martin Luther King Jr. That speech inspired Watkins, while the Freedom Riders who kept rolling into Jackson made him curious.

Following the meeting, just one hour after Dr. King's talk, Watkins and his friend Troy decided to go down to the Greyhound station because, as he said, "We mainly went to see what a Freedom Rider looked like, what a Freedom Rider talked like, how they dressed. I didn't want no part of the Freedom Rider movement. My mama had told me not to get involved, and I listened to my mama." So the two ran across Lamar Street to the Greyhound station with Watkins in the lead, hoping to get a view of the Freedom Riders. Trying to stop their momentum at the door, Troy gave what Watkins remembers as a shove and Watkins ended up inside the terminal. The police immediately grabbed him and asked him where he was born. He told them Milwaukee, his city of birth, though Watkins grew up in Jackson. The police assumed he was an outside agitator and held him.

They kept Watkins in a corner of the station for an hour and then shipped him off to Parchman Farm. They placed him in a cell on death row with murderers where he remained for three days. When Governor Ross Barnett heard that a thirteen-year old was being held at Parchman, he ordered Watkins released to a juvenile court. Watkins eventually received one year of probation and a six-month curfew.

Upon Watkins's release, Bevel came to his house, took him out for a ride, and helped him understand what had happened. As Watkins said, ". . . When I was in Parchman, I didn't really know anything about the struggle. I knew things that we had to do as a Black person. But believe it or not I thought it was a way of life. I'm thinking this is what you supposed to do. . . . So James would take me to different places. I think the first place I was taken was downtown Jackson. And there was two water fountains there. One read White. The other one read Colored. But we couldn't drink from the White fountain."

Bevel took Watkins around to other spots, helping him take in and then reflect on the nature of Jim Crow. The lessons hit home, and Watkins became an activist. He participated in the walkouts at Lanier High School in 1963 and the boycott of the state fair, and later went to work with SNCC in Canton, Greenwood, and throughout the Delta. And Watkins's activist life, a life that led to one hundred arrests, started just with a friend's shove.

Luvaughn Brown and Hezekiah Watkins were not alone. Over the course of the next few years, the Mississippi freedom struggle exploded. Young people stood at the center of this struggle for civil rights. As their stories tell us, Jim Crow was real, a constant reminder of oppression and inferiority, an evil that these kids realized and fought, using all the power of their young lives. The power of the young.

6   The North Jackson Youth Council

COLIA LIDDELL AND THE NORTH JACKSON YOUTH COUNCIL

The Battle of Jackson began in a classroom.

That beginning went like this: Dr. John Salter, a White professor at Tougaloo College, asked students in his American government class to discuss this question: What role should young people play in solving the problems that face their world? The scholars dutifully participated in the conversation that followed, and then they exited at the end of class. One student waited outside the door to speak with the professor.

The lesson held a special meaning for that student, Colia Liddell. In her role as president of the NAACP North Jackson Youth Council, Liddell had already lived an answer to the question Salter asked. Thinking that Salter was a man who lived what his teaching implied, she asked if he would speak at an NAACP mass meeting. Salter quickly agreed. Liddell went on to invite Salter to become the adult advisor to their youth council. Again Salter said yes. This brief conversation was just the start.

Liddell had already started her personal fight to solve those world problems in 1955 when she was fifteen.

As with others in the freedom struggle, she had been affected by the murder of Emmett Till, but she was also moved by the bravery of a young girl in Montgomery, Alabama, Claudette Colvin. At the age of fifteen, Colvin sat in the White section of a segregated Montgomery bus and then refused the order of a police officer to get up. Her action took place nine months before Rosa Parks's more famous refusal.

What had motivated the teenager? Colvin later explained, "I could not move because history had me glued to the seat . . . Sojourner Truth's hands were pushing me down on one shoulder and Harriet Tubman's hands were pushing me down on another shoulder."

That activism sparked a response in Liddell: "Hearing of this girl woke me up. She's fifteen, I'm fifteen."

So Liddell became involved with the NAACP in Jackson, working closely with Medgar Evers. In 1957 she organized the Girls Negro History Club, "trying to get young people involved in learning about ourselves." Remember, this was long before schools nationwide celebrated Black History Month or included much Black history in their curricula.

After entering Tougaloo College at nineteen, Liddell continued the fight. She served as president of the North Jackson Youth Council while her friend Pearlena Lewis served as vice president.

The youth council, invigorated by Liddell's passion, drew new members from local high schools. In 1961 and 1962, numbers increased so much that meetings had to move from a private home to the attic of a local church. Under Liddell's leadership, the young people positioned themselves to play an important role in the struggle to change Jackson.

BOYCOTTING THE STATE FAIR, OCTOBER 1961 & OCTOBER 1962

Salter had probably noticed the youth council in action a few weeks before he spoke at that NAACP meeting. In October 1961, one hundred North Jackson Youth Council students picketed the segregated Mississippi State Fair. At that time, White officials set aside the first week of the fair for Whites and only the final three days for Blacks. During their picketing, the youth council members sang songs and urged their community to stay away, thus demonstrating their refusal to participate in the segregated arrangement.

To quash the council's protest, the police brought in six German shepherd police dogs, charged at the kids, and then arrested seven "for obstructing public sidewalks and streets." But that brutality failed. No one from the Black community came to the Fair the last two days. Those kids had shut it down!

As Liddell shifted her work to voter registration in the Delta, she handed over the youth council reins to Pearlena Lewis, also a Tougaloo student with deep roots in the Jackson community. Lewis took on the leadership, working with Salter and the students.

Lewis knew well the nasty sting of Jackson's segregated society: "As a child, segregation made me feel that I was different, that I was not important, that something was wrong with me." Her family helped her understand that the system, not herself, was the problem. Though she had a quiet nature, Lewis became a strong leader who would take the students into nonviolent battle.

One year later, the youth council repeated its October protest, organizing another State Fair boycott under Lewis's leadership. Lewis helped the council develop thoughtful and effective strategies that made that second boycott another success. To get the word out to the whole Black community, council members called as many people as possible via a phone chain, asking those they spoke with to contact others. The council also publicized the boycott in their brand-new mimeographed newsletter, *North Jackson Action*. One headline announced, "State Fair Is Off Limits." And just in case anyone in Jackson had not yet heard, the youth passed out one thousand leaflets announcing the boycott.

When the fair opened for Blacks, police surrounded the venue, a tactic that likely scared many people away and ironically helped make the boycott a success.

In addition to the police presence, some one hundred young

people gathered at the entrance as they had the year before. They sang freedom songs and chanted, "No Jim Crow Fair for us." Council members spoke with attendees who had not heard about the boycott.

When the Black segment of the fair started on Monday, almost no one attended. That trend continued on Tuesday and Wednesday. Once again, the young people successfully shut down the "Negro State Fair!" More importantly, they made Jim Crow and the civil rights movement fighting against it visible in Jackson, a reality that could no longer be ignored. They fueled a struggle just getting started and ready to ignite. Young people were on the march!

BOYCOTTING DOWNTOWN JACKSON STORES (NOVEMBER–DECEMBER 1962)

After the successful State Fair boycott, the youth council moved next to confront Jim Crow in stores. Members first surveyed their community, finding strong support for a boycott of businesses, and decided to stage one in downtown Jackson during the peak Christmas shopping season.

A *North Jackson Action* article presented the focus of the boycott: "We feel that Negro consumers should start patronizing only those businesses where Negro workers and Negro consumers are treated as they ought to be—as first-class citizens." A boycott leaflet laid out specific demands:

- equality in hiring and promoting employees;
- an end to segregated drinking fountains, restrooms, and seating;
- the use of courtesy titles—Mrs., Miss, and Mr.—when addressing Black customers;
- service on a first-come, first-served basis for all customers—Blacks as well as Whites.

The students knew how to organize. Again they used the *North Jackson Action* for publicity, asking people not to shop in downtown White-owned stores over the Christmas holidays. One headline in caps said it all:

THE BOYCOTT IS NOW OFFICIAL: IS AIMED AT CAPITOL STREET STORES AND OTHER BUSINESSES; IT WILL LAST UNTIL VICTORY; PICKET LINES AND MASS MEETINGS ARE DEFINITELY SET

The students, a mix from college and high school, next created and distributed flyers that trumpeted the boycott. They visited people in their homes, arguing the need for the community to act together. The youth council also worked in local schools, forming boycott committees in Brinkley, Lanier, and Jim Hill high schools.

With all their careful planning and preparation, the council members knew they still needed to do more than just get the word out; they needed to create energy by taking some risks that might lead to arrest and injury. That's where the downtown pickets came in. Those potentially dangerous actions would generate publicity and also put pressure on the store owners.

Though the students in the youth council were eager to picket, some feared that those younger people and their families were too vulnerable. So for the first round of protests on the streets, John Salter, his wife Eldri, and four Tougaloo students whose parents lived out of state stepped up.

On a Wednesday morning in December 1962, the six volunteers rode from Tougaloo to downtown Jackson in bitter cold and "a generally tense silence." Their anxiety grew as they entered downtown and saw the "police cars, motorcycles, and paddy wagons . . . block after block." Their drivers dropped the demonstrators off right in front of the downtown Woolworth's.

The six moved into position, walking in a single line, up and down in front of the store, carrying signs that read "Negro Customers—Stay Away from Capitol Street—Buy Elsewhere" and "We Want Equal Rights for Negro Workers—Boycott Capitol Street" and waiting for the response that was sure to come. It did not take long before around fifty police showed up.

The police captain announced to Salter, "You are under arrest." Salter responded, "Why? What charge?"

According to Salter, "He muttered something about obstructing the sidewalk."

Police arrested all six picketers, took them to the police station, and placed them in segregated cells, releasing some on bond later that day and everyone else the next.

Young people took it from there.

The afternoon of the first action, Lewis and others had staged a rally at Woodworth Chapel on Tougaloo's campus. Half the student body attended. On Sunday of that week, students visited Black churches and explained the reasons behind the boycott. Direct action also continued. Dorie Ladner and another Tougaloo student picketed in downtown Jackson. Police arrested both.

The youth council under Lewis's leadership sustained the boycott through January and into the spring of 1963, keeping up the pressure with more picketing and more arrests. Jackson was coming to a boil.

BIRMINGHAM STEPS IN

While the boycott in Jackson continued, events in Birmingham, Alabama, captured national attention in April and May 1963. Led by the unflappable Reverend Fred Shuttlesworth, demonstrators marched out of local churches and into the streets. They confronted high-pressure firehoses and snarling police dogs. And still they marched.

And then in early May, the children's marches began. The architect of those marches was James Bevel, now with SCLC, who had left Jackson to help out in Birmingham. The kernel of the strategy, the idea of involving young people, likely germinated when Bevel, then with SNCC, recruited kids from high schools and on the streets of Jackson.

Over the course of several days in May, loads of young people stormed out of Birmingham's 16th Street Baptist Church and marched in the streets. Police arrested more than 1,300 young people and adult allies, effectively filling local jails. Americans throughout the country were appalled when they saw the pictures in their newspapers of a dog biting a Black teenager with a Birmingham cop at the other end of the taut leash. Sympathy for the marchers grew.

The power of the children's marches—their persistent courage and dignity in the face of the barbarity of the police response—finally made civil rights a national issue that America could no longer ignore. Young freedom fighters seemed to be marching everywhere.

MAYOR THOMPSON AND MEDGAR EVERS FACE OFF

Meanwhile, with the North Jackson Youth Council engaging in its own actions, older activists in the community took their turn at upping the ante. In May 1963, the Jackson NAACP presented its list of demands to Mayor Allen Thompson.

Thompson responded with a television talk where he made clear that, so far as he was concerned, Jackson would remain segregated. First he spoke directly to the White people of Jackson: "Tonight I want to try to reassure each of you that we are going to continue our way of doing things . . ."

And then he spoke directly "to our 'Nigra' citizens":

You live in a city where you can work, where you can make a comfortable living. You are treated, no matter what anybody else tells you, with dignity, courtesy, and respect.

Ah, what a wonderful thing it is to live in this city.

. . . Now, with these privileges that you have there are certain responsibilities you must assume . . . Refuse to pay any attention to these outside agitators who are interested only in getting money out of you, using you for their own selfish purposes.

Thompson announced that he was ready to meet with "responsible 'Nigra' leaders." Did the Black community wonder what city Thompson was describing? Did they feel angry being spoken to as if they were children?

Eight days later, local TV stations granted Medgar Evers time to respond. In his talk, Evers contrasted Thompson's view of Jackson as a "progressive, beautiful, friendly, prosperous city . . ." with his description of what a Black citizen saw and experienced daily:

He sees a city where Negro citizens are refused admittance to the City Auditorium and the Coliseum; his children refused a ticket to a good movie in a downtown theater; his wife and children refused service at a lunch counter in a downtown store where they trade; students refused the use of the main public libraries, parks, playgrounds, and other tax-supported recreational facilities. . . . He sees local hospitals which segregate Negro patients and deny his staff privileges to Negro family physicians. . . .

Evers conveyed what Black folks wanted:

He wants to get rid of racial segregation in Mississippi life because he knows it has not been good for him nor for the state. He knows that segregation is unconstitutional and illegal. . . . The

Negro citizen wants to register and vote without special handicaps imposed on him alone. . . . The Negro Mississippian wants more jobs above the menial level in stores where he spends his money. . . .

On May 21, the Black community of Jackson held a mass meeting at Pearl Street AME Church to discuss the developing crisis. Six hundred attended. After the people sang and heard speeches by Evers, Salter, and others, a minister read the group's demands. The gathering unanimously accepted the demands and set up a negotiating team. Members of the youth council, however, held no hope for negotiations and prepared for direct action. The push for militancy increased the next day when, as could be expected, the mayor rejected many of the proposed members of the negotiating team, favoring those he felt were more pliable.

After days of back and forth negotiation, some members favored by the community were given permission to attend. Their attendance changed little. Thompson railed against "paid agitators and organized pressure groups" causing the Reverend E. A. Mays, head of the community negotiating team, to tell the mayor, "I don't believe, from the speech you gave, that there is anything in it that will coincide with the things we have in mind." After Mays read the group's demands, all eleven members of the community negotiating team walked out. Jackson headed toward chaos.

THE WOOLWORTH'S SIT-IN (MAY 28, 1963, TUESDAY)

After the negotiations failed, the youth council decided to stage a dramatic sit-in. They chose the Woolworth's in downtown Jackson. Pearlena Lewis and two other Tougaloo students, Anne Moody, twenty-two, and Memphis Norman, twenty, volunteered for action. Moody later recounted these events in her memoir, *Coming of Age in Mississippi.*

That Tuesday turned out to be "hot and muggy."

Adult allies drove Lewis, Norman, and Moody to the Woolworth's in a green station wagon. Norman captured what they all must have felt: "We were all three so afraid. This was the moment of truth."

At 11 a.m., the students arrived at Woolworth's, walked into the store, and bought one item each. At 11:15, they went to the lunch counter.

The three sat toward the middle of the fifty-two counter stools and tried to place an order, but the waitress ignored them. On a slip of paper they wrote down the food they wanted and the total price for their meal, including tax, hoping to hand it to someone waiting on people. Finally, a waitress came over and politely explained that they could be served at the Negro lunch counter. Anne told her, "But we'd like to be served here." The server then shut off the lights and closed the facility.

The few White customers at the counter fled, except for one young woman who glared at the protesters as she finished her banana split before leaving.

Meanwhile outside on the street, police quickly arrested the five who were picketing in support of the sit-in. The three inside Woolworth's appeared calm.

Word about the sit-in got out, and around fifty Whites—high school students, adult members of the White Citizens' Council, thugs, and others—flowed into the store. They surrounded and taunted Lewis, Moody, and Norman calling out "all kinds of anti-Negro slogans" according to Moody. "We were called a little bit of everything." Using pieces of rope, some of the spectators formed nooses and placed them around the protesters' necks. While uniformed police stood outside the store, Lewis, Moody, and Norman continued to sit quietly, facing forward, praying.

And then the violence erupted.

White former cop Bennie Oliver announced, "I'm gonna go

up there and push that Black bastard off of that stool!" He strolled over and punched Memphis Norman viciously in the head, sending him sprawling to the ground. Norman felt pain from that punch the rest of his life. As the Whites cried out support for Oliver, someone else slapped Moody and threw her into a shelf. Lewis was knocked off her stool.

With Norman on the floor, other people started to kick him. Oliver stomped on Norman's head and kicked him in the face, as recorded by a newspaper photographer. The Whites cheered as blood poured from Norman's mouth and nose.

Finally, an undercover policeman stepped forward and arrested first Norman, then Oliver. The Whites' cheers turned to boos at Oliver's arrest.

Only the two females remained. Lewis kept reminding herself, "We're here for a purpose and *it* must be accomplished."

Out in the street, two White supporters—Joan Trumpauer, now a student at Tougaloo after her Freedom Rides, and Lois Chafee, a White instructor at Tougaloo—had realized how dangerous the situation was becoming. They came into the store just as Norman was punched, heading to the counter to join their colleagues. The four women sat.

"Which one should I get first?" someone from the enraged mob asked.

"The White nigger," an old man responded, referring to Trumpauer.

The first speaker, a boy, picked up Trumpauer and carried her out of the store. She turned around and went back inside.

By this time, the White crowd inside had grown to a hundred. Looking for more ways to harass the protestors, they turned to what was on the counter. A White woman pulled open one woman's collar and squirted mustard down her shirt. Others from the crowd followed her example, drenching the protesters with ketchup, mustard, sugar, and everything else they could find. Some toughs dragged Moody from the store, but she too returned to her stool.

Meanwhile, John Salter was at the Jackson NAACP headquarters with Medgar Evers when he heard about the melee. Feeling responsible, he headed downtown, accompanied by NAACP staffer Mercedes Wright and Jackson State College student Walter Williams. All he could think was, "I was the advisor to the youth council. I was the person who more than anyone else had gotten this thing going. If I belonged anywhere, I belonged right there."

When Salter entered the Woolworth's at 12:45 p.m., the scene that greeted him was "surreal, really wild!"

Nevertheless, he sat down with the others. It wasn't long before someone struck him on the head and cut the back of his neck with glass. According to a *Time* magazine reporter, "He stayed hunched over the counter, flinched, but did not fight back when his tormentors poured salt in his wounds."

One from the mob yelled at Salter, "I know you're a Communist." Another screamed, "Worse than that, he's a nigger lover!" Someone hit him with brass knuckles. Freedom Rides veteran George Raymond and eighteen-year-old high school student Tom Beard arrived to join the five already sitting in. Whites in the store continued to drench the protestors with whatever sugar, salt, mustard, and pepper was in the bottles on the counter. The atmosphere was that of a sick carnival. Whites laughed as if they were watching a comedy on television.

Gradually the people in the mob realized they were in a department store filled with all sorts of goods. Someone found spray paint to paint graffiti on the activists' backs. Others grabbed objects off the shelves to throw at and on the protesters. Walter Williams, struck by a heavy object, fell to the floor where he lay moaning, nearly unconscious. Eventually, he slowly and bravely returned to

Walter Williams after being knocked out by a heavy flying object.
Pearlena Lewis sits at the counter.

his seat. Meanwhile, the store's manager sat hunkered in his upstairs office, scared to move.

The assault might have gone on forever if a recently arrived Woolworth's regional manager hadn't shown up. He noted the spiraling chaos, the weak store manager, the lack of police intervention, the ransacking of the store—and maybe even the plight of people sitting in—and acted. He got on the store's public address system and announced, "Woolworth's is now closed." The event had lasted a grueling three hours.

The Reverend Ed King, the White chaplain of Tougaloo College, and Dr. Dan Beittel, president of Tougaloo, also White, escorted the six demonstrators outside, passing through a shower of boos and hurled objects, and into waiting cars. They were driven back to the Masonic Temple where Evers asked Beard, the youngest, why he had risked his life. Beard told him simply, "Somebody had to do it."

Despite all the abuse they endured, none of the protesters who sat in that day responded with any violence.

That evening, the community held a mass rally at the Pearl Street AME Church. It was "wall-to-wall people," anywhere from five hundred to a thousand in attendance. The crowd sang freedom songs and gave a standing ovation to the brave ones who had sat-in at Woolworth's. Many spoke, including Evers, Salter, and Lewis, who called for young people to keep up the fight, declaring, "Ain't nobody gonna turn us around!"

Over the course of the evening, Lewis observed that Evers's "face was lit up." She felt he now "saw the beginning of something he had dreamed about for a long time."

That good feeling was not allowed to last. At midnight, someone threw a firebomb into the carport of the Evers home, but Medgar's wife, Myrlie, was able to put it out. This assault was a sad preview of future attacks against Evers and his family.

As the boycott and the Battle of Jackson continued, young people remained at the center of events. In two days, focus shifted from the stores downtown to the area high schools where teens would rock the city even more.

7 The Children of Jackson March

It was only a matter of time. With so much brewing in Jackson and students at the center of it all, the high schools just had to erupt. Lanier High School in particular owned a reputation for activism. Two days after the Woolworth's sit-in, five hundred Lanier students walked out in protest.

They acted for a variety of reasons. Some expressed support for the boycott of downtown stores and for the brave ones who sat in at the Woolworth's. Bettye Jiles, a senior and a member of the North Jackson Youth Council, explained that the students condemned unjust conditions throughout the city and specifically inequality in the segregated school system. Gene Young, a seventh-grader, argued that the walkout championed the Freedom Riders arrested at Jackson's bus stations. Whatever their specific reasons for walking out, the young people acted with passion.

The students exited at noon, "rushing from the school chanting and clapping for 'freedom.'"

Hezekiah Watkins, an eleventh-grader in 1963, remembers the walkout as a spontaneous event, not necessarily planned or organized. As he recalled many years later,

> We met at the front door and I remember Mr. Buckley (the principal) . . . at the door trying to stop us. Whoever was up front,

. . . just walked on out . . . When the doors opened we all more or less just followed and went on out. We got on the corner. We sang.

The young protesters first congregated on the lawn singing freedom songs, and then many marched around the building, waving American flags and calling out, "We want freedom!" Soon twenty-five intimidating police with dogs showed up. But the crowd got bigger.

The police set up a barricade to keep reporters and parents away. Students started to yell insults at the police. The atmosphere grew more confusing, sometimes party-like and sometimes edging towards violence. Some girls did the twist, a popular dance that year, and others chanted, "Two, four, six, eight! We don't want to segregate!" Others continued to sing, mixing patriotic and freedom songs and even random numbers like "When the Saints Go Marching In."

When a few students threw rocks at the police, the officers responded, chasing the students back into the school. As reported in the *New York Times*, "Negro observers said the police began to push and beat at the students who refused to leave the school yard."

Officers confronted and roughed up at least one mom who tried to get into the building to check on her kids. According to one witness, "They dragged her to a police car and beat her on the legs and in the stomach."

The protest lasted two hours.

At a rally that night, student leaders said they were sorry that rocks had been hurled. At the same time, the children announced they were not ready to stop their demonstrations. Cleveland Donald told the adults, "To our parents we say: 'We wish you'd come along with us, but if you won't, at least don't try to stop us.'" Donald was signaling to the older folks that the marching would continue, that the students would "march to freedom tomorrow." As one young leader told the others, "Bring your toothbrushes, because you're going right to jail."

THE CHILDREN'S MARCH

Though the Lanier High walkout was more or less spontaneous, the marches the next day were carefully planned. Pearlena Lewis, Donald, and other young leaders on the strategy committee called for students from Jackson's four Black high schools to march from their respective buildings at dismissal time. They did just that.

At three o'clock that Friday, May 31, approximately five hundred students from all over Jackson started the long march downtown to Farish Street Baptist Church. It was a one-hundred-degree Mississippi day.

Lewis described the procession plans: "We had informed them to walk in twos from the school. Do not block traffic. Do not swear or use profanity. And don't be violent, whatever happens." The marchers behaved as requested, Lewis noting, "I think it threw [the police] off guard."

David Dennis and George Raymond of CORE had trained the young people in nonviolence, teaching specific tactics to use if assaulted and urging the young protesters to maintain a "relaxed attitude" no matter what happened. Dennis told the students, "We're trying to change a system with love and understanding. It's very difficult . . . maybe it sounds stupid, but if any of you know what violence will accomplish, let me know."

Students marched to the church from all the schools except one. Police stopped the students from Brinkley High School after they had walked only a quarter of a mile of the three-mile trek to Farish Street. The police arrested the leaders and seventy-five more students, hauling them to the Jackson Fairgrounds in garbage trucks. The Fairgrounds had been converted to a makeshift jail, which the police dubbed "Fairgrounds Motel." The students, on the other hand, called the Fairgrounds jail a concentration camp.

Students from the other three schools assembled at the Farish Street Baptist Church as planned. They filled the place up. Inside the church, the Reverend Leon Whitney confiscated any items that might be viewed as weapons, packing the collection plates with pocketknives, sharp pencils, and other suspect objects. As in many civil rights marches, leaders handed each student an American flag that would be a stark contrast to the Confederate flags that would be displayed by the segregationists.

Several people spoke including John Salter, Medgar Evers, and Willie Ludden, the NAACP youth field secretary. Salter later recalled, "The best talks were given by the student leaders themselves. . . . This was their day, and their talks were short and to the point: 'Let's March!'"

At the conclusion of the rally, more than four hundred demonstrators filed out of the church, walking slowly, two-by-two, on the sidewalk, heading toward Capitol Street at the center of downtown. Ludden walked at the head of the line. The marchers waved their American flags as they chanted, "We want freedom!"

As the kids were leaving the church, they could see three hundred law enforcement officers just two blocks away, nearly one officer for every marcher. Jackson police stood in the front of that army. According to Salter, "They stretched from the buildings on one side of the street straight across to the buildings on the other side, rank after rank after rank of them. Their blue helmets, their clubs, their guns glinted in the hot sunlight." Next came Mississippi highway patrolmen in brown helmets with riot guns and then sheriff's deputies. Behind all of them stood the garbage trucks. It must have been a terrifying sight! But how terrified the police must have been by those teens to think they needed such overpowering force!

Through his bullhorn, one cop announced that anyone without a permit for marching would be arrested. A few frightened students started to run, and police chased them, firing into the air. The rest of the students marched steadily forward toward the barricade of police.

Jackson police captain John L. Ray stopped Ludden at the police line and asked him, "Where are you going, young man?"

Ludden told him, "Sir, I'm headed to the federal building."

When Ray asked him if he had a parade permit, Ludden responded, "I'm not parading."

Looking beyond Ludden to all of the young people standing behind him and still coming out of the church, Ray inquired, "Where are all those people going?"

"You'll have to ask them," Ludden asserted.

After a few more rounds of back and forth, Ray exclaimed, "You and your people had better turn back or go to jail!"

Ludden kept moving forward when he heard another police officer call out, "Nigger, where the hell do you think you're going?"

The officer hit Ludden on the head with his nightstick and then kicked him repeatedly until he passed out.

Still, the young people continued up the street, waving their American flags and chanting as they moved right into that wall of police. Officers responded by tearing flags out of the marchers' hands.

Next came the arrests.

The process was methodical. Most students just stood and waited to be arrested, though, as the *New York Times* reported, "they shouted at the police: 'We want freedom, yea!'"

Police threw the children into county farm trucks, police vans, and garbage trucks. Ludden, now barely conscious, won a garbage truck: "I was tossed into the truck like a piece of trash and crashed against the floor of the container. It was a filthy stinking pit. The garbage truck had not been cleaned after the day's haul. . . . It was a sunny, hot day and there was no ventilation." The kids pounded on the insides of the garbage trucks as they were driven away.

Some of the arrested were transported in police vans. Marcher Shirley Harrington-Watson remembered how the police locked the doors to the van and turned up the heat on that already scorching day. The vehicle was so hot, her clothes stuck to her skin and left an imprint.

But Dennis and Raymond had trained those young people well. Despite all this mistreatment, faced with injustice, brutality, and humiliation, the children behaved as nonviolent warriors, allowing themselves to be arrested and showcasing their moral superiority.

The march ended in a matter of minutes. Evers stood on the sidewalk watching, undoubtedly proud of his children but also shocked at the cruelty of the police. The World War II Army veteran remembered: "Just like Nazi Germany . . . Look at those storm troopers."

Police took most of those arrested to the State Fairgrounds, separating boys and girls and then placing them in the livestock pens surrounded by barbed wire where everyone slept on the concrete floors usually used by farm animals. Workers served the students food that had been mixed in garbage cans. The kids told Salter, "The police shoved some of the students around, spat in the water buckets, threw food on the ground." Conditions were awful.

But despite their terrible situation, the young peoples' spirits remained high. They sang freedom songs and chanted.

Lewis had served as a march organizer, but she had not participated in the protest. Still, she felt a sense of responsibility to the young people and went down to the Fairgrounds that night, gaining entry in order to pray with her colleagues. Once there, Lewis led the kids in the singing of freedom songs. Police then arrested her and took her to the Hinds County Jail with other march leaders. That day, six of the seven Lewis children were arrested.

Governor Ross Barnett expressed approval for how Mayor Allen Thompson had handled the protests and offered him use of the infamous Parchman Farm if there was a need to arrest more protesters.

Other authorities, however, wished to wipe their hands clean of the entire day and decided to allow parents to take their children home that night. To leave the Fairgrounds prison, all the kids had to do was sign a statement declaring they would not participate in more protests. Most chose not to sign and remained in the makeshift jail.

A MASS RALLY, A SLOWING DOWN, AND MORE PROTESTS

The evening of the children's march, NAACP executive director Roy Wilkins arrived in Jackson. At a press conference, Wilkins noted, "In Birmingham, the authorities turned the dogs and fire hoses loose on peaceable demonstrators. Jackson has added another touch to this expression of the Nazi spirit with the setting up of hog-wire concentration camps. This vindicates the NAACP contention that Mississippi officials regard the Negro citizens of this state as animals, not human beings and fellow citizens . . ."

That evening, fifteen hundred people from the highly energized Jackson community held a mass meeting. Some of the students who had been released from jail showed up and received a "thundering ovation." After Wilkins spoke, one brave eight-year-old challenged him, asking if he was "willing to go to jail for freedom." On the spot, Wilkins responded, "I'm with you all the way!"

The day after the children marched, Thompson issued a statement, bragging that the city could "handle 100,000 agitators if pressure groups want to send them there," meaning he would throw those "agitators" into jail. It was a brave boast, but the fear tactic did not stop the protests.

More action took place the next day. Wilkins and Evers picketed in front of Woolworth's and got arrested. Wilkins carried a boycott sign reading, "Don't Buy on Capitol Street." Because of

Medgar Evers at his office in the Masonic Temple building near the campus of Jackson State College.

that message, police charged the protesters with restraint of trade, a crime requiring a $1,000 bail. Wilkins was infuriated. Not happy with direct action, he paid his fine, got out of jail, and, boarded a plane back to New York.

The children persisted. Later that same day, having seen the spirit of the young people, Salter helped organize another march. Around one hundred and fifty students left the Masonic Temple and headed toward downtown. Some had been arrested the previous day and had just been released from the Fairgrounds.

From their porches, people in the surrounding community watched, some joining in behind the young people. At first, there were no police in sight, but soon sirens blared.

The marchers veered down side streets to avoid the police, but, when more cops and two garbage trucks arrived, the march came to an end. Police arrested eighty-eight more people, again throwing them into garbage trucks and hauling them down to the Fairgrounds.

As the trucks rode by, people on the street heard something familiar from inside: freedom songs. With the marchers gone, police turned on and beat some bystanders.

While all this direct action was heating up in Jackson, the national leadership of the NAACP wanted to slow things down—for several reasons. The national NAACP tended to be a cautious organization. Things were different in Mississippi where leaders like Evers accepted more active protests. The national organization generally did not support direct action, preferring to work through more traditional means of legal and legislative initiatives. It also felt particularly uncomfortable with so many children landing in jail. So the NAACP leadership maneuvered to squelch the marching, changing the structure of Jackson's strategy committee and manipulating it to dump committee chairs Salter and Lewis.

On Monday morning, the young people and others, expecting another march, came to the NAACP offices in the Masonic Temple. But NAACP staff told them that there would be no more immediate mass demonstrations.

This lack of support for direct action in Jackson and the unwillingness to provide bond money for those jailed slowed but did not stop the protests. On Monday, June 3, Moody and six others picketed in front of the J. C. Penney department store, right across the street from Woolworth's. Moody ended up in Hinds County Jail.

On Tuesday, twenty-eight youth and four adults staged demonstrations along Capitol Street, picketing and sitting-in. Police arrested all thirty-two.

Many protests took place in a short time, and many would follow. Between May 28 and June 5, 1963, there were 1,048 arrests for civil rights activities in Jackson. With all those arrests, the continuing sit-ins, picketing, church kneel-ins, and more, and with students' determination to keep the movement alive despite the NAACP's push to slow down, it looked like nothing would stop the young people of Jackson.

Then, one despicable action took the wind out of everybody's sails: Medgar Evers was murdered.

8   A Tragedy and a People's Reaction

· ·

THE PRESIDENT RESPONDS

After months of struggle and what probably felt like little progress, something positive greeted the community. The evening of Tuesday, June 11, 1963, President John F. Kennedy finally responded directly to all the danger and risk and heartache civil and voting rights activists had faced. Millions watched as he delivered an important speech on national TV. Until that moment the president had acted cautiously, but now, prodded by the marches, pushed by the sit-ins and Freedom Rides, affected by the examples of Medgar Evers, Ella Baker, and Martin Luther King Jr., and moved by the people in the streets crying out for justice, Kennedy took a stand:

"The events in Birmingham and elsewhere have so increased the cries for equality that no city or state or legislative body can prudently choose to ignore them. . . . I am, therefore, asking the Congress to enact legislation giving all Americans the right to be served in facilities which are open to the public—hotels, restaurants, theaters, retail stores, and similar establishments"

The proposed legislation would address and hopefully end the worst aspects of Jim Crow segregation that the freedom fighters had exposed and condemned and risked their lives to oppose. In a reversal of the call and response singing in many African American churches, the congregants—the people—called, and the preacher— President Kennedy—responded.

During the day, Medgar Evers had been excited about the

upcoming presidential address. He called Mrs. Evers and reminded her to watch that evening, knowing he would be out on NAACP business and would hear the president speak while away from home. Mrs. Evers and the children listened to the address, the children staying up late so they could greet their dad when he got home. As Mrs. Evers listened, she felt that Kennedy "was talking directly about our Capital Street boycott, our voter registration drives, . . ." His words were in part a vindication for her husband's passion and dedication. As she said, it "made what Medgar was doing seem more important than ever before." The Civil Rights Bill that emerged from Kennedy's speech more than a year later represented a major victory for Evers, but it was a victory that neither the president nor he would live to see.

A Major Tragedy and a Community Gathers

After a long exhausting day that ended with a mass meeting, Evers headed home just after midnight. Waiting eagerly for his return, Mrs. Evers and the children were excited when they heard the car pull into the driveway and the engine turn off. Their excitement quickly turned to terror when they heard a gun blast. Mrs. Evers bolted to the driveway and found her husband on the ground, crawling toward the door, blood all around. Neighbors raced over, one rushing Evers to get medical attention, but it was too late. Medgar Evers died forty minutes later in a nearby hospital. He was thirty-seven.

Avowed racist and Ku Klux Klan member Byron De La Beckwith Jr. had hidden behind a bush across the street from the Evers' home and fired his rifle, martyring one of the movement's greatest leaders.

Jackson's simmering rage began to boil.

The news spread quickly. Pearlena Lewis had been with Evers that evening, attending the mass meeting and afterwards heading to a social gathering. At 2 a.m. Johnny Frazier knocked on the door and delivered the awful message. Lewis remembers, "It hurt so deep, but it just made me more determined."

Anne Moody, staying with Dave and Mattie Dennis, heard the news report on TV at 12:30 a.m. "We just sat there staring at the TV screen. It was unbelievable. Just an hour or so earlier we had all been with him."

Colia Liddell, who had been participating in a voter registration drive in Selma, happened to be at Tougaloo when she got the word. She quickly began to prepare Tougaloo students to march.

The next morning, fourteen Jackson ministers, leaving from the Pearl Street AME Church and intending to go to city hall, marched two by two in silence. Spaced apart they were merely walking on the sidewalk and not "parading," which, without a permit, was illegal. Despite that careful approach, after only two blocks, police arrested all fourteen.

Meanwhile, many young people arrived at the Masonic Temple. Observing the gathering, John Salter concluded, "They were ready to move and there was nothing that anyone could do to stop what was now going to occur." So, at around one o'clock, Tougaloo's Reverend Ed King offered "a prayer for Mississippi," and then two hundred persons exited the Temple, turned left toward downtown, and advanced down the sidewalk. Half of the two hundred were students from Tougaloo College and kids from around Jackson, those youthful activists loved most by Medgar Evers.

They headed down Lynch Street, marching on the sidewalk in twos and threes as they sang freedom songs. Right away the protesters spied a hundred city, county, and state police officers carrying "riot guns and automatic rifles." The officers stood just one block ahead. As spectators started to occupy lawns and then the sidewalks, the marchers stepped into the streets and walked to within a few feet of the law officers. Lynch Street grew silent.

The police began moving forward, and then they bulldozed

Young men being arrested during the Jackson children's march, riding in the truck and heading to the makeshift jail at the state fairgrounds.

the marchers, clubbing them and hustling them toward waiting garbage trucks as spectators chanted, "Freedom! Freedom! We want freedom!" Police arrested one hundred and forty six people and drove them to the Fairgrounds. More than half were under the age of eighteen.

Back in the neighborhood, people stood along the sidewalk and on their lawns, continuing to sing and staring in anger as the police paraded up and down the street.

That evening five hundred attended a mass meeting at the Pearl Street AME Church. Dave Dennis and some Jackson ministers spoke, encouraging the continued use of direct but nonviolent action and the boycotting of downtown stores.

Then Mrs. Evers, whose husband had been murdered just hours earlier, addressed the crowd. She told the five hundred,

I come here with a broken heart. I came because it is my

duty. . . . It was [Medgar's] wish that this movement would be one of the most successful that this nation has ever known . . . I hope by his death that all of you here—and those not here—will be able to draw some of his strength, some of his courage, and some of his determination to finish this fight. Nothing can bring Medgar back, but the cause can live on.

People wept. At the meeting's end, everyone sang "We Shall Overcome," including reporters from the national media. Not so reporters from the local press.

As for other White Jacksonians, the *Times* reported, "Whites in the strongly segregationist community publicly expressed shock. But privately they showed more concern over the possibility of Negro retaliation." One policeman told a reporter, "We're just scared to death. That's the truth."

Leaflets passed out that night called for people to return the next day, "prepared for action." But as the community planned, some ominous signs arose. The *New York Times* noted "well-founded reports that a number of Negroes had armed themselves." Tension mounted.

PROTESTS CONTINUE

On Thursday, June 13, the temperature again hit one hundred degrees.

Dorie Ladner and Anne Moody headed over to Jackson State College where they tried to recruit students for a march scheduled for later that day. Though the two did not meet with much success at Jackson State, more Tougaloo students did head into town. Another day of protest was shaping up.

At Pearl Street AME Church, the young people preparing to march first received instruction in nonviolent action from Dave Dennis. The marchers then left the church, just after noon, waving

American flags and turning left, away from town, in an attempt to sidestep the police. More than one hundred law officers confronted the young people anyway. Spectators again came out of their houses and lined the streets.

After warning the marchers to disperse, police pulled flags from their hands and forced them into police vans and garbage trucks, arresting another eighty-two and taking everyone down to the Fairgrounds. Salter remembers that "The faces of the police, as they began to tear the American flags from the hands of those who carried them, were filled with raw hatred. And there was hatred in the eyes of the people who watched this."

Moody, arrested with the others, remembered bitterly how the police stashed the young people in vans and turned on the heaters, holding many for two hours.

Despite the force and intimidation, the people from the neighborhoods continued to support the marchers. Folks throughout the area chanted, "Freedom! Freedom! We want Freedom!" as police hauled the young people away. Now the police were getting really scared. Noting the people's angry determination and their growing identification with the marchers—and probably fearing another Birmingham or Montgomery, where entire communities stood up against Jim Crow—they wondered when those strong emotions would turn into actual violence in their own city. Jackson Deputy Police Chief John Ray called three times for quiet on his bullhorn and then for the streets to be cleared. The police quickly moved toward those watching, harassing many, arresting some, and assaulting others. Finding Salter on a house porch with Dorie Ladner and others, police saw an opportunity to punish a man they knew and despised. They beat Salter bloody and then arrested him for disturbing the peace and resisting arrest.

Still, Salter managed to make it to that evening's mass meeting. Wearing his torn, bloody shirt, he received a standing ovation when he entered. He spoke, encouraging the crowd to keep up the pressure by continuing to march.

When Salter referred to pressure, he meant nonviolent pressure, but calls for a more violent approach hung in the air. One minister, pointing to the police brutality, told Mayor Thompson, "People are buying guns. They are mad. They want to shoot. We're trying to hold it down." One bystander who witnessed the events that day told a reporter from the *Times,* "If Mayor Thompson don't want no violence he better stop his little boys in blue helmets from beating people up. And that don't mean violence next week. It means violence right now!"

On Friday there was another gathering in Jackson, and Salter was surprised to see so many new faces. Those faces belonged to SNCC members, the young people who had been working with leaders like Bob Moses and organizing in towns throughout Mississippi, especially in the Delta. Despite the word "nonviolent" in SNCC's name, its members added a sense of militancy to the protests.

HONORING AND REMEMBERING MEDGAR EVERS

On Saturday, June 15, Jackson would hold a funeral for Evers at the Masonic Temple with a march to follow. Given his service during World War II, Evers would be buried in Arlington National Cemetery, just outside Washington, D.C., national recognition he deserved. But he had also served the people of Mississippi. The local community needed an occasion to reflect on and honor the man.

White authorities agreed to the march, but it was to be silent— no singing and no chanting. Many expressed frustration with that mandate for silence, and some called for a demonstration to follow the march, one that would allow the community to honor Evers in a fitting manner, that would express that deep anger so many felt over the assassination, over the police brutality, and over the injustice experienced daily throughout Mississippi—a demonstration that would demand the justice that Evers had fought for his entire life.

It would also be a demonstration Jackson police viewed as illegal. Three days after Evers's murder, five thousand assembled inside the Masonic Temple for his funeral. One thousand more stood outside. People had come from all over the state, an indication of the impact Evers had on all Mississippians. According to Salter, who asked people around him where they came from,

> They told me, naming places besides Jackson: big towns, little towns, rural hamlets all over Mississippi. There were people from the Delta and from the hills in northeastern Mississippi, from the Gulf Coast area, and from the pine country down in the southeastern part of the state.

Dr. Martin Luther King Jr. attended, though he was not invited to sit on the stage. Tension between the NAACP and Dr. King's Southern Christian Leadership Conference undoubtedly drove that decision. In fact, the NAACP national leadership tightly controlled every aspect of the event, down to the purchase of clothes for the Evers family. Some activists were infuriated because the NAACP used the occasion to promote itself, an action they felt showed disrespect for Evers.

The service started at eleven o'clock and lasted for an hour and a half. Local ministers spoke, and then Roy Wilkins offered a well-crafted eulogy:

> For a little while he loaned us and his people the great strength of his body and the elixir of his spirit. . . . If Medgar Evers could live in Mississippi and not hate, so shall we, though we shall ever stoutly contend for the kind of life his children and all others must enjoy in this rich land. . . . The bullet that tore away his life [also]

tore away at the system and helped to signal its end. The opposition has been reduced to clubs, guns, hoses, dogs, garbage trucks,
and high wire compounds. . . . Obviously nothing can stop the
drive for freedom.

When Wilkins concluded, all in the Temple sang the powerful,
"We Shall Overcome." At the end of the service, a minister read the
instructions from Jackson officials that mandated "a silent mournful
funeral procession," and then everyone reconvened outside.

That June 15 was another hot day in Jackson, the temperature
over a hundred degrees for the third day in a row. Salter recalled, "It
seemed infinitely hotter than I had ever known in my life, and my
clothes were soaked with sweat." The overall climate was more than
hot. Moody, watching the funeral assemble from a hill across the
street, commented, "As the pallbearers brought the body out and
placed it in a hearse, the tension in the city was tight as a violin string."

Five thousand walked a mile and a half from the Masonic Temple
to Collins Funeral Home on Farish Street. Young people from the
NAACP youth groups, SNCC, and CORE marched silently at the
rear, while dignitaries, including Roy Wilkins and Martin Luther
King Jr., marched at the front of the line. The marchers stretched
out for four blocks. They would walk for two hours.

As the people moved into a White area of Jackson, Salter noted
that those residents "stood in front of their houses and business
places, women and children standing behind their men. There was
shock and hatred and fear mixed on all of their faces; but they were
silent and so were we."

Of course, law enforcement officers maintained a heavy presence that day. Salter remembers that "solid walls of police, rank
after rank, had formed a cordon through which we passed." As he
walked by the heavily armed police, Salter "could see the hatred
in their faces."

The experience of marching though Jackson—past those hate-filled White neighborhoods and the masses of police clutching their weapons—must have wreaked havoc on the already intense emotions in the community.

As the front of the line reached the funeral home, a minister told the people to disperse.

As the young people in the rear crossed Capitol Street, those from SNCC, the NAACP youth groups, and CORE started to sing, "We Shall Overcome." But they then continued in silence the few more blocks up Farish Street

When the young people arrived at the funeral home, that mandated silence ended. Someone began singing another song, "Oh, Freedom!" Others joined in, violating the rules set by officials. Then that first singer broke into "This Little Light of Mine." More began to sing and clap. They belted out the line "all over Capitol Street, I'm gonna let it shine" three times, pointing toward Capitol Street. Misconstruing the gesture as an indication of where marchers would move next, police headed toward Capitol Street to defend it, a maneuver that ironically created room for the marchers to head toward Capitol Street. As they moved down Farish, "other persons spilled out of the small shops, taverns, and restaurants along the street and fell in behind them." One thousand now marched

The young people and their supporters had walked a block and a half when they encountered a barricade of two hundred and fifty police. The activists stopped, penned into a one-block area.

Deputy Chief Ray got on his bullhorn and shouted, "Your leaders said you wanted to have a silent, mournful march. We agreed under those circumstances." He then ordered the throng of one thousand to disperse. Someone yelled, "We want the killer! We want the killer! We want the killer!" Others in the crowd stomped their feet and chanted "Freedom! Freedom! Freedom!" A "staccato cadence" drove the chant. Both the volume and the anger increased.

Seeing things slipping out of their control, police responded in their usual brutal manner. Officers with dogs appeared, forcing people down the street, viciously beating some, smashing one man in the face with the butt of a rifle, clubbing a woman, and just grabbing others for arrest.

As police sealed in the marchers, some in the crowd started throwing "bricks, bottles, and other missiles." The sound of growling police dogs and crashing bottles filled the air. Colia Liddell looked up and saw "on tops of buildings. . . . Blacks lined up with guns hanging over the edge."

Ray again shouted on his bullhorn: "You came here to honor a dead man and you have brought dishonor! You have brought dishonor! You have brought dishonor!" The protesters did not respond to Ray's absurd accusation. But when some officers drew their weapons, the demonstrators yelled back, "Shoot! Shoot! Shoot!" A local newsman heard one county policeman say to another officer, "We may as well open fire. If we don't do it today, we'll have to do it tomorrow!" A massacre was in the making.

Suddenly, John Doar, a White official from the United States Department of Justice, stepped forward and "walked into the sealed-off block of Farish Street with bottles and bricks crashing around him." He told the crowd, "'This is Mr. Doar with the Justice Department. You're not going to win anything with bottles and bricks!'"

Quickly, Dave Dennis stepped up to help Doar. Dennis approached the crowd and requested calm, asking one kid to lower his gun and another not to heave a brick. Willie Ludden from the NAACP grabbed Ray's bullhorn and told the people, "'This man is right. . . . Go home!!! That's the best you can do now!'" The marchers paused, thought, and gradually moved on. Still, the police arrested twenty-seven people, including Dorie Ladner, and took them to the Fairgrounds.

Though calm had been restored, the potential for violence had not ended. One man standing in a doorway explained, "The only way to stop evil here is to have a revolution. Somebody have to die."

THE AFTERMATH

Fearing more protests and wishing to restore order, President Kennedy intervened the next day, June 16, and pushed Mayor Thompson to negotiate with the Black community. He told Thompson, "I think the problem is to see what it is we can get the Negro community to accept . . . without any of these riots.'" Sad to say, at this time the president wanted only to defuse the immediate situation, not to end the conditions that led to the protests.

In response, Thompson offered the following: the hiring of six Black police officers and eight Black crossing guards in Black neighborhoods, the promoting of eight Black municipal workers, and the freeing without records of the young people arrested in demonstrations. Not much. There would be no changes in segregated facilities, no biracial committee for solving problems in the future. In exchange for little, the community had to agree to stop mass protests. The Black ministers, wishing to be conciliatory, accepted the terms.

That night, the ministers presented those terms to the rest of the community at a mass meeting of three hundred. The leaders worked hard at the gathering to sell the agreement as the best deal for the moment, using their own position in the community as clout, invoking the name of Medgar Evers, and suggesting there could be more direct action down the road if things did not improve. Begrudgingly, the community accepted the terms.

Dorie Ladner later said, "We were infuriated at the agreement, but it was clear the mayor was not willing to negotiate in good faith. We accepted it under duress. Otherwise, there would have been all-out war and likely more loss of life." The *Times* reporter at the meeting echoed Ladner's sentiments: "It was clear that although older Negroes were inclined to accept the mayor's terms, younger Negroes were in a mood to continue their protests."

Through the intervention of the NAACP's national office, the direct action phase of the Jackson movement slowed down, but the fight for civil rights and justice did not come to an end for the young people of Jackson. The day of the funeral, James Forman, executive secretary of SNCC, announced that it would have ten field secretaries in Jackson to help sustain protests there, though they soon had to leave the city as an organization when the NAACP cut them out of planning. In reality, activity shifted elsewhere in the state, mainly to the Delta, followed by many of the young people who had been engaged in the direct action in Jackson. Disappointed with the NAACP, they joined SNCC and headed to other parts of Mississippi to continue their march toward justice.

As for Evers's murderer? Following the pattern for such actions at that time, Byron De La Beckwith Jr. was tried by all-white juries two times in 1964 and each trial ended in a hung jury. He was viewed by many segregationists as a hero. Thirty years later, things had changed in Mississippi, new evidence was presented, and De La Beckwith was tried a third time and found guilty. He died in prison in 2001.

Elders III—The Saga of Fannie Lou Hamer

· ·

TRICKING A CHILD (1923)

Not far from the wooden shack where she lived, six-year-old Fannie Lou Townsend (her later married name was Hamer) played by the side of a gravel road. Mr. Brandon, owner of the plantation where Fannie Lou's family sharecropped, drove up beside her and leaned out the window. He asked, "Can you pick cotton?"

"I don't know," she responded.

He corrected her. "Yes, you can. I will give you things you want from the commissary store."

And then Brandon named all of the treats Fannie Lou could receive if she did as he asked. The list included Cracker Jack, sardines, a quarter-pound of cheese, and gingerbread cookies. The items were tempting to a little girl who often went to bed hungry, a little girl who "didn't hardly have food to eat; didn't have clothes to wear."

And to receive those treats, all the six-year-old had to do was pick thirty pounds of cotton.

So little Fannie Lou marched out into the field and joined her mother, her father, and her nineteen brothers and sisters. The parents accepted what was to be and told their little girl she was welcome to join them, but she had to pick the thirty pounds on her own. That she did.

Fannie Lou worked all week, picking the cotton and filling and refilling a cloth flour sack with the required thirty pounds. Brandon was good to his word, providing the promised treats and telling Fannie Lou to return the next week.

And the next week she picked sixty pounds.

At six, Fannie Lou's childhood was already starting to end. As she recalled, "So I picked the thirty pounds of cotton that week, but I found out what actually happened was he was trapping me into beginning the work I was to keep doing and I never did get out of his debt again." That work is called sharecropping, an economic and social system mentioned previously. For sharecroppers, as Fannie Lou stated, "Life was worse than hard. It was horrible."

Despite the brutal nature of sharecropping, Fannie Lou managed to go to school through sixth grade. She loved school, she loved learning, and, in particular, she loved reading. Her great wish was "to get a real good education and to go some place else to get it!" This was never to be and no surprise, given the unrelenting demands placed on sharecroppers.

THE SHARECROPPERS' LIFE

The system of sharecropping grew up after the Civil War. The Thirteenth Amendment had abolished slavery, so plantation owners needed a new way to organize the planting and harvesting of cotton, as well as to keep African Americans working and subservient. Sharecropping accomplished all of these purposes.

Sharecropping worked this way. The plantation owner provided land, seed, animals, and equipment so sharecroppers could plant, in addition to an advance of money so families could survive, though just barely. The sharecropper families worked the fields and then gave the owners a part of the cotton they harvested, with the other portion of the cotton then sold in the sharecropper's name. Because of the portion they often received, some sharecroppers called this system "halvin'."

Sharecroppers worked from "daylight to dark," from "can to can't," the week stretching from Monday to Saturday night. The work was grueling and the weather unforgiving. The Mississippi Delta, where Hamer grew up and lived, was stifling hot.

And children worked as sharecroppers. As Hamer reminds us, "Yes, I worked in the fields. In fact, all the kids around in this Delta worked in the fields."

Despite their backbreaking labor, sharecroppers lived in abject poverty. The Townsends were no exception. According to Hamer, "We never did have enough to eat, and I don't remember how old I was when I got my first pair of shoes, but I was a big girl. Mama tried to keep our feet warm by wrapping them in rags and tying them with string." Sharecroppers lived in cabins or shacks, not unlike the homes their enslaved ancestors had lived in.

Plantation owners kept the sharecroppers in constant debt. The

Sharecroppers photographed by Dorothea Lange during the Great Depression.

money the sharecroppers made when their crops were sold was rarely enough to pay back what the owner had advanced. Some owners kept the often illiterate sharecroppers in debt through out and out cheating. To pay off their debts, the sharecroppers were forced to stay on the land and continue this cycle year after year.

Sharecropping was a mean system. The owners and other White people needed a way to explain to themselves and others why something so mean and unjust might actually be all right. First, they embraced the myth that Blacks were inferior to Whites. Hortense Powdermaker was a White anthropologist who studied Indianola, Mississippi, during the thirties. In a survey she administered to White citizens, 84 per cent of the respondents agreed with this statement: "Negroes are innately inferior to White people, mentally and morally." Powdermaker also shared what she discovered about the prevalence of Black stereotypes: "The belief is general among White people that the Negro is congenitally lazy and must be kept in debt in order to be made to work." Such beliefs formed the foundation for the entire system of sharecropping, as well as the system of Jim Crow laws we have been discussing.

On the other hand, the owners did not know how the people they treated so wretchedly really felt. According to Powdermaker, "The average White person in this community seldom realizes the extent to which this group [Blacks] questions his superiority." That questioning, likely, helped people in the community challenge the system that kept them down.

HAMER AND SNCC (1962)

In 1962, Fannie Lou Hamer and her husband Perry "Pap" Hamer had worked on the Marlow plantation for eighteen years. The plantation was outside the Delta town of Ruleville, a town in Sunflower County. First Hamer worked as a sharecropper, and then she worked as a timekeeper. The timekeeper kept track of how long people worked, the worth of what they had picked, and, overall, how much they had earned.

That year, SNCC came to town. When Mary Tucker got involved with SNCC, she thought of her old friend Fannie Lou. Tucker offered an invitation:

> And I said, 'Fannie Lou, I want you to come to my home.' She said, 'What for Tuck?' I said, 'I want you to come to a meeting. We're having a civil rights meeting. . . . We're learning how to register and vote so you can be a citizen.' She said, 'Tuck, they taught us that mess in school and that's turned me off like that.'

Hamer later regretted how she had spoken to her friend, asked forgiveness, and attended a SNCC meeting at William Chapel Missionary Baptist Church.

James Bevel, a Freedom Rider we met previously, and James Forman, SNCC executive secretary, spoke that night about voter registration. Few Blacks in Mississippi could vote in 1962. Here is what Hamer learned at William Chapel:

> And I went to the church, and they talked about how it was our right, that we could register and vote. They were talking about we could vote out people that we didn't want in office, . . . That sounded interesting enough to me that I wanted to try it. I had never heard, until 1962, that Black people could register and vote.

Hamer was forty-five in 1962.

The idea of voting people out of office had particular appeal to Hamer given that ". . . the man that was our night policeman here in Ruleville was a brother to J. W. Milam, which was one of the guys helped to lynch this kid Emmett Till."

At the meeting Bevel asked for volunteers to go down to

Indianola, the county seat, so they could register to vote. Hamer was one of the eighteen who said yes: "When they asked for those to raise their hands who'd go down to the courthouse the next day, I raised mine. Had it up as high as I could get it."

HAMER TRIES TO REGISTER

That next day Hamer got on a bus and rode down to Indianola. When they arrived at the courthouse, the volunteers were a little nervous and reluctant to go in. At first they just stayed on the bus. Charles McLaurin, the SNCC field secretary who accompanied them, relayed what happened next: "Then one little stocky lady just stepped off the bus and went right on up to the courthouse and into the circuit clerk's office. I didn't know this was Fannie Lou Hamer." The others followed.

Hamer continues the story:

> . . . so when we got there, there were people there with guns and just a lot of strange-looking people to us. We went on in the circuit clerk's office, and he asked us what did we want; and we told him what we wanted. We wanted to try to register. He told us that all of us would have to get out of there except two. So I was one of the two persons that remained inside, . . . We stayed in to take the literacy test.

As a part of the test, the registrar asked Hamer to talk about the sixteenth section of the Mississippi state constitution. According to Hamer, that was a section "dealing with facto laws and I knowed as much about a facto law as a horse knows about Christmas day." Needless to say, Hamer did not pass the test. Whether she could have interpreted the Mississippi constitution probably would have made no difference. Sometimes the questions were as ridiculous as how many bubbles are in a bar of soap? White voting registrars were given great latitude to decide who passed literacy tests and who didn't. Whites, even ill-educated ones, usually passed; Blacks, even high school and college graduates, usually did not.

Everyone got back on the bus and rode back to Ruleville. On the way home, the highway patrol stopped the bus and fined the driver for driving a yellow bus. This was one more form of harassment that scared everyone, but a voice on the bus helped to soothe their fears. Hamer started to sing, songs like "Down by the Riverside," "Ain't Gonna Let Nobody Turn Me Around," and "This Little Light of Mine." Singing was to become one of Fannie Lou Hamer's trademarks. On this first occasion, her voice calmed the people as they joined in.

HAMER GETS FIRED

In addition to the literacy test, Hamer had had to fill out a form with twenty-one questions that sought personal information including her name, address, and place of employment. Registrars often turned the information over to the White Citizens' Council, which would inform employers who could then decide how they wanted to respond. As Hamer said, "Well, see, when you put by whom are you employed, you fired by the time you get back home."

So, when Dee Marlow, the plantation owner, heard what Hamer had done, he came down to her house and demanded, "Fannie, you've been down there to Indianola to register today, didn't you?"

"Yessir, Mr. Marlow, I sure did."

"Well, if you want to stay here and everything go like it always is, you better go back down there and get your name off that book."

Hamer told him, "Mr. Dee, I didn't go down there to register for you. I went down to register for myself."

Hamer left the plantation and her home.

That evening Hamer attended a voter registration meeting in Ruleville where she told the people present she had been thrown off the plantation and had nowhere to go. Her friend Mary Tucker said, "Don't say you ain't got nowhere to stay as long as I got shelter—if I ain't got but one plank, you stick your head under there too!'"

In the fall, Hamer returned to the registrar and told him, "Now, you cain't have me fired because I'm not livin' in no White man's house. I'll be here every thirty days until I become a registered voter."

On December 4, 1962, after SNCC literacy classes and one more attempt to register, Hamer correctly interpreted the Mississippi Constitution for the registrar, passed the test, and gained the right to vote.

Hamer joined SNCC and eventually became a full-time field secretary, working to help others register. In 1964, she addressed the Democratic National Convention, which we will discuss later.

9 Greenwood Part 1—
Sam Block Shakes Things Up

· ·

Like so many other Black youths, Sam Block could not get Emmett Till out of his mind. He told an interviewer, "What made me realize that I had to do something was when Emmett Till was killed." And there were also people who drew Block into the movement.

Growing up in Cleveland, Mississippi, Block got to know Bob Moses's mentor, Amzie Moore, who was a friend of Block's family. Moore helped Block realize he could do something about the conditions that allowed for Till's murder and for the murderers to go free. Block said about Moore, "He was a man that I really respected because he was the only person in Cleveland who was really addressing any issues. . . . So I spent a lot of time talking to Amzie . . ." The talk had impact.

In June 1962, Bob Moses invited Block to work for SNCC in Mississippi to organize a voter registration drive. Block quickly accepted, choosing Greenwood, just forty-five miles up the road and in the county where Till was murdered.

Moses drove Block to Greenwood and asked some tough questions on the way: "Now, Sam do you know that the possibility is that you could be killed?" Block told him he did. Moses pushed again, stating, "Okay, but I want you to be sure you really want to go into Greenwood." Block again said yes, "So Bob dropped me off in Greenwood. . . . I had no car, no money, no clothes, no food, just me." Block was just twenty-three and in a haven for the White Citizens' Council.

Block found a place to stay in Greenwood, and then he hit the streets. "I would go canvassing, just talking to people in the community . . . sort of testing the pulse of the people. Hanging out in the pool halls, wherever people were, the laundromat, . . . the grocery stores. . . ." First Block listened, and then he slowly introduced the subject of voter registration.

Block soon discovered that "there were a lot of angry people in Greenwood." They were still angry because of what happened to Emmett Till and angry about the murders of other Blacks in the county, about which authorities did nothing.

But the community was not so sure about this stranger. As Block reported, "When the people found out what I was there for, they said it was best for no one to have anything to do with me . . . because . . . I was going to stir up trouble and be there for a short length of time, and then leave." A lot of people thought that's what SNCC did in McComb, that they shook things up there and then pulled out.

And where the Black community met Block with genuine skepticism, Whites met him with vicious brutality. Still, Block didn't quit.

BIRTH OF A MOVEMENT

Eventually, Block found allies from Greenwood's older generation. He connected with Cleveland Jordan, a World War II vet who made the local Elks Club available for voter registration meetings and took the young organizer under his wing. "Mr. Cleveland Jordan sat me down and gave me a whole history of what had been going on in Leflore County. He told me about how he had decided to start a voter education movement [Leflore County Voters' League] in the early fifties. He gave me the names of those persons who were involved in the League and the names of those he felt were still interested in getting a voter education movement started." Several of those old activists became the first people in Greenwood to work with Block.

So Block made some progress. That progress did not last, however, as fear slowed the momentum. Block managed to hold one meeting at the Elks Hall, attended by around twenty people. At a second meeting the people sang freedom songs, but the singing got Block kicked out of the hall, the Elks fearing that White authorities would identify them with civil rights "agitators." And then Block's landlord figured out he was in Greenwood to start a voter registration movement and asked Block to leave the apartment. He found a car in a local junkyard and for a week slept in that car. Eventually he found a new residence.

Nothing about Greenwood was easy for Block. SNCC could not afford to pay him, despite his pleas to the SNCC office in Atlanta, and he was sometimes forced to eat out of garbage cans.

But through sheer grit and persistence, the movement grew—in fits and starts. Block connected with the Reverend Aaron Johnson, who opened his First Christian Church to SNCC's voter registration meetings. At the first meeting, Jordan introduced Block to the community:

> Well, we got somebody now that is going to help us do something. We have been wanting somebody, now here he is. I want you all to give him all the support that you can. Don't be scared of him. Treat him like he is one of us because he is. We have been living in fear, afraid to do something. It is time to do something. The time is now.

Block again led the people in song. This time nobody minded. Block possessed a nice singing voice, and music became a big part of the gatherings he organized. The people loved the songs. According to Block, "The next day as I walked the streets I met a lot of people and the thing that they remembered most about the meeting was the songs we were singing. And they asked me when were we going to have another meeting and sing those songs. And I began to see the music itself as an important organizing tool to really bring people together." Block was laying the foundations for a voter registration drive. Greenwood needed such a drive. Leflore County's Black population was twice the White population, but of the thirty-three thousand Black residents, only two hundred and fifty could vote.

After a second mass meeting, Block took twenty-one people down to the courthouse to register to vote. None of the twenty-one successfully registered and, when they headed out, they ran into the sheriff.

Deputy Sheriff Wardine Smith—"Big Smitty"—confronted

People lining up at the Leflore County Courthouse in Greenwood to register to vote.

Block outside the courthouse and fired off this ugly question, "Nigger, where you from?"

When Block said Mississippi, Smith refuted him. ". . . I know you ain't from here, cause I know every nigger and his mammy."

Block challenged his slur. "Well, you know all the niggers, do you know any Colored people?"

The deputy then spit on Block while waving a pistol in his face telling him, "Nigger, let me tell you one goddam thing. I don't want to see you 'round here the next hour, the next minute, or the next second. I want you to pack your goddam bags and I want you to leave Greenwood, Mississippi."

Block told him, "Sheriff, if you don't want to see me around here the next day, the next hour, the next minute, or the next second, the best thing for you to do is to pack your bags and leave because I am going to be here." Block reported, "Big Smitty just dropped his hand and gun in amazement."

The people took notice.

Block and others drove the twenty-one back to their homes, followed by the police. As the people got dropped off, the officers wrote down the names of everyone who had come down to the courthouse, hoping to intimidate them. That failed. Block's bravery touched people deeply. Those who had gone down to the courthouse shouted back at the police, "You don't scare me no more. You don't scare me no more!"

Throughout the rest of the summer, the voter registration drive in Greenwood continued and Block met with more small successes, finding an office for SNCC, obtaining some local financial backing, and continuing to bring small groups down to the courthouse to sign up to vote, even though the registrar used the literacy test to keep many from actually registering. Block also recruited Dewey Greene Jr., a member of a prominent Greenwood family. Dewey became an important colleague for Block.

With age-old fears embedded in the Black community and White pushback, Block's persistence was necessary. Violence continued to challenge Block's work and test the will of others in the movement.

THE CYCLE: PROGRESS AND RESISTANCE

Bob Moses saw that Block could use some help and in the middle of August sent him eighteen-year-old Luvaughn Brown from Jackson and Lawrence Guyot, a Tougaloo student. The three worked hard, connecting with members of the community and generating a small cadre of volunteers, mainly teenagers, who went door-to-door, encouraging those they spoke with to go down to the courthouse to register. Despite that fear felt by many in the community, the number of people attempting to register increased.

But as the movement grew, so did White resistance. A few days before Brown and Guyot arrived in Greenwood, a man from the local White Citizens' Council called Block and told him, "If you take anybody else up to register you'll never leave Greenwood alive." Block did continue taking people to register. Soon after the call, he was walking down the street and three White men leapt out of a Ford van, grabbed him, took him to a vacant lot, and beat him.

Greenwood police followed Block everywhere he went.

One night Block, Brown, and Guyot met in the second floor of SNCC headquarters to discuss their progress in the voter registration drive, as well as the fear they encountered out in the community. About 1 a.m., Block called Moses to make his daily report, looked out the window, and saw a police car with an officer talking on the radio. The three started to watch the streets more carefully.

Soon a car pulled up and White men holding guns, ropes, and chains emerged. The three heard someone coming up the stairs and then banging on the door. They decided to flee, sneaking out a back window onto the roof of a next-door cafe, then shimmying down an antenna pole, hitting the ground, and making it to the home

of Clarence Jordan's son, David, where they again called Moses.
When Block returned the next day, he found the office a
shambles, most of their files missing, and Moses and Willie Peacock,
another SNCC organizer, asleep on the couch.

White authorities hounded the landlord until SNCC was
thrown out of its office.

Despite the violence and intimidation, Block knew SNCC had
to persevere to build a movement; SNCC needed to show the community it meant to stay. Peacock agreed to join Block in Greenwood.

As the months moved forward, folks in Greenwood started to
trust SNCC because the activists were sticking it out and becoming more a part of the community. Locals put up SNCC workers
in their homes, and SNCC found a new office and set up shop.

In early fall 1962, the weekly mass meetings had increased in
size, drawing from thirty to fifty people. Speakers like Moses and
Fannie Lou Hamer energized the meetings, and more people headed
down to the courthouse to register.

Block and Peacock made a point of recruiting teens, and the
young locals continued to join up. As Block recalled, "We would
spend time at the little restaurants where they hung out and go
around the school campus, Broad Street High School, talk to people
and get them involved."

Block built a movement in Greenwood. He hunkered down
with Peacock and a growing band of activists who all watched
Greenwood come alive.

Backlash followed.

WHITES IN GREENWOOD GET MEANER; THE MOVEMENT GROWS

Whites in town did not like all of the agitation, and they
schemed. Just before winter, the all White Leflore Board of Supervisors stopped the distribution of surplus food that came from
the federal government—the food that sharecroppers had come

to depend upon during winter. The supervisors claimed that the administrative cost for the distribution process was too high, but, in truth, the cutoff was retaliation against civil rights activities. The supervisors did not seem concerned that families, including children, might starve.

But the cruelty of the White Supervisors backfired. SNCC worked to compensate for the loss, distributing food to the angered and energized community, food that had been donated by people from the North and elsewhere. The food distribution brought more people into the SNCC office where they could learn about voter registration and channel their anger.

After that failure, White backlash increased. On February 20, 1963, arsonists burned four Black businesses. When Block told a reporter that the arson was a failed attempt to destroy the SNCC office, authorities charged him with "making statements calculated to breach the peace." Block was tried, convicted, and sentenced to six months in jail; it was his seventh arrest in the seven months he had been in Greenwood. Block appealed the conviction. Blacks in Greenwood had turned out for Block's trial to support a man they had come to trust and respect.

And then later in February, violence showed up again. One evening, a white Buick followed the SNCC car driven by Jimmie Travis as it headed out of Greenwood down a country road. Bob Moses and a third activist sat next to Travis. Here is Travis's description of what happened:

> The car continued to follow until there were no other cars in
> sight, and then pulled up alongside of us as if to pass. At the time,
> I thought they were going to throw something at us or try to run
> us off the road. I felt something burn my ear and I knew what
> they were doing. They had opened fire on us . . . it sounded like
> a machine gun. I yelled out that I had been shot, as I let go of the

wheel. Moses grabbed hold of the wheel and brought the car to a stop on the shoulder of the highway. I was scared.

The shooting left thirteen bullet holes in the SNCC car and one bullet in Travis. Moses rushed Travis to a nearby hospital and later to one in Jackson where doctors removed the bullet. Travis survived.

Recognizing the message Greenwood Whites had delivered, Moses concluded, "the only way to answer this kind of violence: instead of letting up—to pour it on; instead of backing out, to move more people in. " And then from early March to mid-April 1963, forty organizers from all over Mississippi flooded into Greenwood. And more people headed to the courthouse to register—two hundred and fifty during the first three weeks of March. Mass meetings at the Reverend Johnson's church and churches throughout Greenwood attracted "large crowds."

From Sam Block's solitary entrance into the town, the movement in Greenwood emerged and flourished. Greenwood became a part of a growing Mississippi movement, as voter registration projects evolved in other Mississippi towns including Hattiesburg, Greenville, Clarksdale, and Ruleville, where Fannie Lou Hamer had become involved in the movement. COFO, the Council of Federated Organizations, was created in Mississippi to coordinate the work of all civil rights groups active in the state, including SNCC, NAACP, CORE, and SCLC.

And despite the unrelenting opposition of segregationists and white supremacists, SNCC and other activists did not waver. They watched a reluctant community become an emboldened community ready to confront the evil it faced. And young people stood at the core of the struggle.

10   Greenwood Part II—The Children
· ·

JUNE JOHNSON: A TEENAGER JOINS THE FIGHT

June Johnson felt the sting of Jim Crow as a child. Her mom, Belle Johnson, worked as a cook at a nightclub, and June sometimes went along to help, eating at the club, generally in the kitchen. One night, tired of devouring her hamburger in the back, she walked out into the restaurant and innocently sat at the bar. Mrs. Johnson had to school June, telling her, "Baby, you can't sit out there, we are not allowed to do this. You will get me in trouble." June was learning that certain places were open only to White people.

Like her parents, June knew hard work. In September and October, all throughout her childhood she went out to the fields to pick cotton. June found her life dreary and monotonous. "We didn't have anything to be into. We really, really didn't. Picking cotton and chopping cotton was a way of life."

But the year that Sam Block came to Greenwood, the year June turned fifteen, her life started to change.

SNCC COMES TO TOWN

In late 1962 June noticed something new in Greenwood: "My sister and I and about three other girls was walking from school and we saw these men passing out leaflets, stopping us at the high school and all. From Broad Street to where we lived on North Street they was all down on most of the corners passing out leaflets, you know telling us to come out to mass meetings . . ." Those men were SNCC organizers.

In the days following, as June walked to and from school, she made a point of passing the SNCC office and stopping in to see Bob Moses, Block, Luvaughn Brown, and others. She was starting to get just a little excited.

For June's mom, SNCC was something to worry about. First of all, Mrs. Johnson could easily get fired if June became an "agitator" and her boss found out. Second, June was already getting herself into trouble and did not need any more opportunities! June held a reputation for fighting with other kids and for arguing with authorities like her teachers, as well as her mother. She also took no guff from White people. Once, when she was picking cotton at the age of ten, a foreman took his hoe and struck her bottom to push her to pick more, but June just smacked him right back.

June realized the SNCC office created a new way to act up, despite any consequences. "So I guess I was the headache. I would always slip away and go down there to see what was going on. . . . I knew I was going to be punished, but it was a curiosity."

JUNE BECOMES INVOLVED

One day on the way to school, June bumped into Moses. It was early, 8 a.m. As June said, "I would run into him and he would chat me. I was a very inquisitive person. By nature, I like people. . . . My interest had basically somewhat drifted away from school because I was so curious about what this man was saying to me and what was going on." When she asked Moses why he had come to Greenwood, he said "they were there to make sure that Blacks became first-class citizens, and they wanted us to get involved, help canvass the community, pass out the leaflets, ..."

June listened—then she looked for more ways to become active. She needed to be a little sneaky where her parents were concerned, but still, more and more often, she would head over to the SNCC office to go out with others to canvass neighborhoods and talk to the adults about registering to vote. And she started attending mass meetings.

Though Moses encouraged June's involvement as he walked with her to school, her teachers, like many African American adults who knew what could happen to any Black person who stood up for civil rights, spoke against her activity, and she in turn talked harshly about her teachers. "They were trying to suppress our minds in terms of how we thought about what was going on." Adding to her teachers' dismay, June grew an Afro: "So we started wearing our hair natural. And my particular teacher stated to me that she would actually pay for me to get my hair done. And I told her you know that I liked it the way it was."

June's commitment deepened when she participated in a spring conference in Atlanta. Before she could attend, Moses had to convince her mom to let her go. Belle Johnson felt some hostility toward the movement activity, but she liked and trusted many movement people like Moses, Annell Ponder, and Block, so she agreed. The conference promised adventure for June, who "had never been out of Mississippi in my life." In Atlanta, she met and listened to activists talking and explaining. Upon her return, June spoke—reluctantly because she had little experience with public speaking—at a mass meeting to describe what she had learned at the conference.

Initially, her mother did not know the extent of June's involvement, but, as June persisted, Mrs. Johnson came to see what was happening in Greenwood with her daughter and with the broader community. She gave in a bit as she developed a greater respect for the civil rights activists in town.

Nightmare in Winona

So much about the movement had been uplifting for June, but harsh danger lay ahead that would challenge those good spirits. In

1963, she traveled to South Carolina to attend a literacy-training workshop with Ponder, Fannie Lou Hamer, and others. At the conference June met the legendary Septima Clark—the "Mother of the Movement," in Martin Luther King Jr.'s words—and learned about literacy education and nonviolent protest. This training would empower June to teach basic literacy skills to enable people to pass the tests that would allow them to register to vote.

On the way home, the bus with the activists on it stopped in Columbus, Mississippi, so riders could eat. June and several others sat at the White counter, but they did not get served. Then when June and Hamer moved to get back on the bus, planning to sit in the front, the driver shoved them to the ground and called them "niggers." He made them wait to let the White passengers board first. The Black activists eventually did board, sitting toward the middle, but they also complained about their treatment and told the driver that they would file a lawsuit against him.

On his way down the highway, the driver stopped and made some calls. The bus soon arrived in Winona, a town less than thirty miles due east of Greenwood. When five from the group of activists got off, including June, they saw the highway patrol and groups of "White folks" hanging around the station, seeming to be waiting for June and her comrades.

The five went inside the station, sat down at the lunch counter, and asked for service. June continues, "The White woman was rude and nasty and she told us that they didn't serve niggers and that we would have to get up and move and go to the other side."

They continued to sit until the police entered, surrounded them, and threw them out. Outside, Ponder started to take down the license numbers from the officers' cars. That act was the last straw. The police arrested all five, including June, and took them to jail.

In the meantime, Hamer had waited on the bus to rest her legs.

But when she saw what was happening to her friends, she came off the bus, so the police arrested her as well.

Those arrested faced mortal danger.

Inside the jail, the police started to confront the activists one-by-one. First they "interrogated" June. According to June,

> The state trooper took us inside the jail.. He opened the door to the cell block and when I started to go in with the rest of them, he said, 'Not you, you black-assed nigger.' He asked me if I was a member of the NAACP. I said yes. Then he hit me on the cheek and chin. I raised my arm to protect my face and he hit me in the stomach. . . .
>
> Then the four of them—the sheriff, the chief of police, the state trooper and another White man threw me on the floor and stomped on me with their feet. They said, 'get up, nigger.' I raised my head and the White man hit me on the back of the head with a club wrapped in black leather. My dress was torn off and my slip was coming off. Blood was streaming down the back of my head and my dress was all bloody. Then they threw me in the cell.

Next the police beat Ponder with "blackjacks, and a belt, fists, and open palms." Their purpose, according to Ponder, was that "They really wanted to make me say 'yes, sir' . . . and that is the one thing I wouldn't say." According to historian John Dittmer, Ponder "emerged with her head bloody and swollen, a tooth chipped, and her clothes torn."

James West, another rider, was the next to be beaten by the highway patrolmen and fellow Black prisoners.

The worst assault was saved for Fannie Lou Hamer. Another Black inmate was brought in to administer the beating. As Hamer stated, "that man beat me till he give out."

But supporters learned where the five were and soon came from

Greenwood and elsewhere to work on their release. It took three days, but they managed to get everyone out.

Mrs. Johnson had come to Winona from Greenwood to get her daughter. She was glad to have June back, but also likely scared and angry when she saw what the police had done. According to June, "My eyes were closed literally. My head was busted wide open. My face was bruised very badly. And my body had scars all over."

The entire world would soon hear about the cruel violence of those arrests and beatings. The following August of 1964, Hamer described publicly, in matter-of-fact but horrifying detail, what happened in Winona to her, June, and the others. Hamer presented this story when she spoke in Atlantic City, New Jersey, at the Democratic National Convention. Carried on network television, Hamer's words electrified the nation. For most White people, it was the first time they had heard an African American describe directly the brutal treatment they received in Mississippi when

Addressing the 1964 Democratic National Convention, Fannie Lou Hamer told how she was beaten in the Winona jail.

they asserted themselves, a narrative that contradicted America's "the land of the free" motto.

After what had happened in Winona, Mrs. Johnson no longer forbid June's participation in the movement. In fact, seeing what her daughter had endured, she also became involved. Quitting her job in the restaurant, she became the head cook for SNCC. She also started to canvass, encouraging her neighbors to register so they could vote. Belle Johnson opened her home to SNCC members and became legendary amongst the young activists for her hospitality and wonderful cooking.

The incident in Winona did not deter June, either. It just fired her up.

The once fearful June spoke to a crowd in nearby Itta Bena, urging them to register to vote so they could kick out of office those officials "who beat you up for nothing." In August of 1963, June went to the March on Washington. While she remained active with

Fifteen-year-old Annie Lee Turner, defiantly nonviolent, being dragged across the pavement by police during a Greenwood Freedom Day.

the movement, she "was constantly in and out of jail," lending support to store boycotts and Greenwood Freedom Days, and helping to ensure that "the movement rocked on, rocked on, rocked on!"

Up to her death in 2007 at the age of fifty-nine, June Johnson continued her activism, working as a paralegal for Legal Services in Greenwood and later in Washington, D.C., for the municipal child support enforcement agency.

EMPOWERED: THE STORY OF ENDESHA IDA MAE HOLLAND

Throughout American history, Black women and Black girls have been victims of sexual assault—one of the cruelest aspects of Jim Crow life. Endesha Ida Mae Holland was one of those who suffered. When she was eleven, babysitting for a White family, Ida was taken upstairs to a bedroom where her employer raped her. Eleven years old. But she decided not to tell her mother, thinking, "What was the point?" Nothing would be done. She accepted that "if you were Black, you were always at the mercy of White people." Many years later Holland told *People* magazine, "It happened to a lot of girls."

At the age of thirteen, Ida became a prostitute on the streets of Greenwood. Then her life got even worse. When a newspaper-wrapped bottle of whiskey slipped from her hands and broke on the high school grounds, the principal expelled her. Kicked out of school in ninth grade, Ida survived as a prostitute, as a shoplifter, and finally as a prison inmate. At that point, Ida, known to her friends as Cat, saw little that was positive in herself or hopeful in her future.

But events soon challenged those bleak assessments.

FINDING SNCC

Rent was due. Cat Holland, eighteen and out of prison, knew how to get the needed money. She spotted a "nicely dressed, clean-looking Black gent" and followed him, calling out "I got it—come an' git it—." The "gent" just kept walking, leading Holland to a brick building with a sign that displayed a Black hand and a White hand clasping, a sign announcing that the building contained the Greenwood office of the Student Nonviolent Coordinating Committee. A lot of people were standing around. Holland had stumbled on SNCC's food distribution project, the one replacing the federal government food surplus program that had been eliminated by the Leflore County supervisors to punish the community for its civil rights activity.

The man Holland had followed turned to the crowd milling around outside the office and announced, "We need help to get all these people signed up. Who can read and write and is willing to help us with this task?" Egged on by a friend who knew her literacy skills, eighteen-year-old Holland walked inside with that "clean-looking Black gent" —Bob Moses.

Inside the office, Holland walked past a woman who typed fast and did not look down at her fingers. Holland was surprised because she "had never seen a Black woman use a typewriter" and assumed the woman was typing gibberish. She could not believe that a Black person could actually type. But Holland looked over the typist's shoulder and saw the woman "hadn't missed a word!"

Holland knew very well how she and other Black women were treated in Greenwood and had assumed it was something to do with the low capabilities of Black people. The world has a way of teaching one's status in any society. In Greenwood, for instance, the telephone directory placed a "Miss" before the names of White women. Not so Black women. At the time, Holland didn't know that Black people, including herself, deserved more respect.

She spent that first day helping sign people up so they could receive food, but those who signed also agreed to go down and register to vote.

Other people praised Holland for her work that day, and she felt herself changing inside, if only just a little. She noted, "Being treated with respect was something wholly new for me."

From that point on, Holland's involvement in SNCC grew steadily. She continued to sign people up and help distribute food. Then she started teaching people basic literacy so they could fill out forms and register to vote. And soon she went out canvassing, talking to people about going down to the courthouse so they could register.

She attended the mass meetings where people sang, recognizing that "the mass meetings were the things that held us together." She described one such meeting where "Sam Block spoke first. He talked about our right to vote, as citizens of this country, and about our fears—which were real, but not enough, he said to keep us from the franchise. When he finished, there was not one dry eye in the church." Then Willie Peacock led the crowd in singing "This Little Light of Mine."

As he did with so many, Moses helped Cat Holland see her "little light" in a new way. As she said, "He would always have something good to say about everybody and included me, about how brave I was. . . . And what a freedom fighter I was."

HOLLAND MARCHES

And then Holland began to march, first after Block was arrested and then one month later when someone shot two rounds of buckshot into the home of Dewey Greene Sr., head of a respected Greenwood family that had become active in the movement. That shooting outraged the community, and the next day one hundred and fifty people marched in the streets.

The marchers walked past city hall to protest the assault on the Greenes and then moved down to the Leflore County courthouse so people could register to vote. Holland joined the protest, finding it difficult to believe someone could threaten the Greene family.

The protesters proceeded through "jeering White onlookers" and up to police wearing riot gear and carrying shotguns. The officers also brought an intimidating German shepherd, and Mayor Charles Sampson threatened, "I'll give you two minutes to get out. . . . If you don't, we are going to turn the dog loose!" No one moved. Even when the dog tore at Moses's trousers, he stood fast, despite his phobia of dogs.

But when the police started to kick the Reverend David Tucker, her mother's minister, Holland warned the police, "Don'cha kick him!" She went to grab the officer, who immediately arrested her. "Here, take this nigger to jail," the policeman ordered. As Holland said, "That was the first time I was arrested for the movement." It would not be the last.

Police kept Holland in the back of a squad car until Chief Curtis Lary came by. He knew Holland from previous encounters and let her go, telling her to stay away from those "outside agitators." She didn't listen. Upon her release, she walked straight back to the SNCC office.

The thing Holland remembered most from that day was Lary's expression: "The look on Chief Lary's face gave me a sense of freedom at that very moment. . . . He had never before seen us Blacks act this way. And at that moment . . . the indecision on his face said he didn't know what to do. And that gave me a sense of power."

THE MARCHING CONTINUES

The next day, Thursday, one hundred people went down to the courthouse to register. Holland led the march of forty-two who returned from the courthouse and headed to Wesley Chapel; Tucker was beside her at the front of the line. The police were out in force, with "auxiliary" officers (other Whites from Greenwood) beefing up the thirty-man police department. According to the

New York Times, "Roughly dressed Whites stood on the sidewalk and muttered threats."

Again the police brought their German shepherd, and some "White bystanders" called for the police to "sic" the dog on the marchers. Police obliged. The dog lunged viciously and bit Tucker, drawing blood.

Next week, the people marched again. Forty members of the community paraded on the sidewalk and then headed to the courthouse to register. When Lary demanded that they disperse, Holland responded, "We will not." The police arrested nineteen people.

For Holland, marching led to prison. Police arrested her thirteen times over the course of the Greenwood movement. Of course, she had been in jail before, but "it didn't seem so much like a cell to me this time when I went back for civil rights. I didn't realize then that I did have a purpose." In fact, her jail experiences energized Holland: "I was always raising my hand to go to jail. That kind of became my forte."

Holland recalled one time when she was at the notorious Parchman Farm for thirty-three days. When she got out, she rode through several towns while people cheered her as she passed, and then, when she entered a mass meeting at Turner Chapel, she received an ovation.

Many people helped Holland to see her life in a complete contrast to its start, but most important was Moses, who became her guide. "We all would have followed Bob Moses to the end of the Earth. And that's the truth."

Beyond Moses, Holland was affected by women in the movement. Amazed by people like Anne Moody and Dorie Ladner, she wanted to be like them. People from Greenwood got to her as well, such as Belle Johnson, June Johnson's mom who had originally opposed her daughter's activism. When Belle Johnson marched, she "walked with this sense of pride. We would try to imitate as we walked . . ."

The movement gave Holland self-respect and a feeling of power: "I had always wanted to be somebody. I didn't know what I wanted to be. But the civil rights movement gave me this chance." She also stated, "For the first time, I had committed myself to a cause greater than myself—one I was willing to fight, even die for . . ."

Holland completed her GED and attended the University of Minnesota, eventually earning her doctorate in American Studies. Dr. Holland had a career in academia, serving as a professor and teaching at two colleges. She also became a playwright. Her most famous work was a play about her own life, *From the Mississippi Delta,* later also the title of her memoir. She died in 2006 at the age of 61.

The movement changed more than the structure of society; it also changed individual people in profound ways, reshaping the way they thought about themselves, the way they lived, and their place within the world. Holland's life reflects such transformation. As she said, "If you've been a ho', be a doctor, too."

SILAS MCGHEE BECOMES INVOLVED

Several factors drew Silas McGhee into the Greenwood movement, but nothing influenced him more than his mother: ". . . the only role model that I had was my mother . . . ," he stated. Laura McGhee was one tough lady, and, after Emmett Till was killed just ten miles away, she told her children, "I don't care what you do. If you make it back home, I will not let nobody come to this house and take you away. I will *die* first!"

With such a strong presence in his life, McGhee needed only some gentle prodding to become an activist. When the sit-ins in Greensboro, North Carolina, became news, McGhee ". . . would always think about what it would be like if that did happen here in Greenwood." He did not have to wait long.

At eighteen, McGhee watched Mississippi explode with the

Freedom Rides. Then Sam Block came to Greenwood, and the town erupted with its voter registration campaign. McGhee connected with that drive when a sympathetic teacher discussed voter registration in class. To help the students learn more about it, the teacher suggested that McGhee observe the marches and report back to class. The observations accelerated McGhee's civil rights education.

Then he attended 1963's March on Washington for Jobs and Freedom.

GOING TO THE MOVIES, PART 1

One year after McGhee graduated from high school, Congress passed the Civil Rights Act of 1964, legislation that legally ended segregation in public facilities. President Lyndon Johnson signed the bill on July 2; McGhee acted several days later.

McGhee lived on a farm outside of Greenwood and walked the three miles into town alone. His purpose? Integrate Crystal Grill, a local restaurant. But when he arrived, the restaurant was closed.

Still, after such a long hike, McGhee remained determined to test the new law, so he changed targets and headed for the Leflore Theatre, one of Greenwood's two White movie theaters. McGhee marched up to the window and asked for a ticket. The teller first checked with the manager and then sold McGhee his ticket. He went in, sat about five rows down from the back of the theater, and watched Jerry Lewis's *The Patsy*, which he later called the "sorriest movie I have ever seen."

But he didn't have to watch the whole thing.

Around forty minutes into the film, four White teens came in and sat behind McGhee, one asking, "What is this nigger doing up here?" They made other remarks, dumped popcorn down his back, and then left. Soon they returned to confront McGhee again, demanding that he leave. McGhee continues: "And the guy who was in front of me grabbed me by the collar and jerked me out of my seat. And when he did that I hit him in the face. I ran out in the aisle and kicked the other two. I was mad. I ran into the lobby."

McGhee went into the manager's office and refused to leave until the police arrived. They took McGhee to the station and questioned him, wanting to know who put him up to going to the theater. McGhee told them he developed the plan on his own. The police drove him home and lectured him, reminding McGhee that he was from a good family. At home his mom offered her support, but his brother Jake offered a rebuke: Why didn't Silas share his plan so Jake could have joined him? Silas and Jake became comrades in the integration effort and made several visits together to the LeFlore.

GOING TO THE MOVIES, PART 2

For the next visit to the Leflore, Jake had to go alone; his brother was not available because he was speaking to the Clarksdale NAACP about his earlier trip to the Leflore. At his first attempt to integrate the theater, Jake got beat up, but the assault did not daunt the McGhee brothers! They continued their forays to the movie house, prompting retaliation in this small-town environment.

On Thursday, July 16, Silas McGhee was walking in Greenwood when three men accosted and forced him into a car at gunpoint. What must he have been thinking at that moment? They took him to an abandoned garage where one asked, "You the nigger that's been going to the movies? Ain't you been taught better than that?"

They went after McGhee with pipes and sticks. But McGhee picked up a shovel, defended himself, and escaped, "bleeding from head wounds and suffering from shock." The FBI later arrested the three men, the first to be charged with violating the new Civil Rights Act.

Then on a Saturday night in late July, the McGhee brothers visited the Leflore one more time. On this, their fourth attempt to integrate the theater, they watched *The Carpetbaggers*. This time, no one bothered them inside the movie house, but when they stepped outside, they saw a mob. Silas recalled, "it was White people, White people, White people as far as you could look across the bridge, . . . Nothing but car lights and cars. They were all lined up. People out there blowing their cars, hollering, shouting, and telling us to come out."

Cars were backed up to the Yazoo River Bridge. The McGhees couldn't get a cab, so they called the SNCC office. SNCC sent out two cars, one as a decoy. Not knowing the plan, Silas and Jake saw the decoy and fought their way through the crowd to get inside. The crowd saw their opportunity and assaulted Jake as he climbed in. Then a bottle flew through the air and broke the windshield. Flying glass cut Silas, and the driver had to take him to the hospital.

The mob followed, and in the hospital, hoodlums made sure Jake and Silas did not feel safe. As Silas recalled, "They were beating on the windows, they was beating on the doors. They had to lock the hospital up because they were trying to get in. And they wouldn't let us out." The sheriff came, but he said there was nothing he could do.

Hearing what was going on with her two boys, Mrs. McGhee and her son Clarence, on leave from the army, rushed over to the hospital. Clarence called his commanding officer who called U.S. Attorney General Robert Kennedy. The McGhees waited three hours for Kennedy to get back to them, but, when he finally did, he told them they would be going home within thirty minutes. In six minutes, the sheriff and highway patrol arrived, cleared out the mob and escorted the McGhees home.

McGhee Shot

After that scary event, violence continued to trail Silas McGhee. One day a police officer threatened him, and that night someone shot him.

McGhee had been driving SNCC members to Lula's Cafe so they could attend a good-bye party for visiting students from the Freedom Summer. He was sitting in the car outside Lula's when gentle rain started, and he fell asleep. A white pickup drove by and someone in it fired a rifle out the window. McGhee was shot in the head. The bullet broke his jaw and traveled down his throat.

When his colleagues heard the blast, they ran outside and opened the door. McGhee fell out. Several SNCC colleagues drove him to the hospital, Bob Zellner tearing off his shirt to bandage the wound as Linda Halpern held McGhee's head in her lap. She recalled, "My dress became soaked with blood"

They got to the hospital only to be told they had come to the "wrong" entrance. The police and doctors told them, "This is for Whites only. You're at the wrong door." No doubt anxious to get McGhee help, they went to the Black entrance and started to bring him in. Then the guards at the door stopped them because Zellner was not wearing a shirt! By herself, Halpern dragged McGhee in on a stretcher. As Halpern went down the hall of the hospital, she heard the police saying, "Hey, they got that nigger Silas tonight. He was a big one." Hearing more threats, she grew even more fearful. So SNCC arranged for a helicopter to transport McGhee to a hospital in Jackson, where he spent ten days.

He not only survived but continued working in the movement after his release. Then in 1966 McGhee was drafted into the army. Upon his return to Greenwood, he found the Leflore Theatre closed, driven to economic ruin from a boycott by Whites who had been angered by what they saw as the management's caving in to the mandates of the 1964 Civil Rights Act. Today the theater site is a parking lot.

Silas McGhee returned to the farm where he was raised, working several government jobs over the years. He lives on that land today.

Despite his brushes with death, McGhee views the movement

with a playful spirit, perhaps more playful than many other activists express. He recalled, ". . . we were just happy-go-lucky. We would go to demonstrate, we would sit in, go to the movie and have a good time."

FINAL THOUGHTS ABOUT GREENWOOD

As the capital of Mississippi, Jackson experienced its rightful share of civil rights activity, but it did not stand alone. In fact, the movement in Jackson was a spark that then spread fire throughout the state. Greenwood is prime evidence of that spreading. Its powerful movement, the courageous activists and young people who laid their safety and their lives on the line in a refusal to accept the status quo, changed much about how African Americans lived in that town and saw themselves. They experienced a new sense of pride, discovered a new feeling of empowerment, and realized long-denied dignity.

Sam Block had entered town alone, like a cowboy sheriff from the old movies, coming into Greenwood to bring law and order—in his case, justice. The steadfast nature of Block and others, the gentle charisma of Bob Moses, and the persistence of SNCC provided the call, but the people in the community responded and stepped up into leadership roles. Think of Endesha Ida Mae Holland going from prostitute to professor through the movement, June Johnson changing from troublemaker to a disciplined rebel for the cause, and the McGhee brothers deciding on their own to integrate the Leflore Theatre.

When the people of Greenwood rose up in struggle, they changed not only Greenwood but incited change in the rest of Mississippi. One of those towns ignited by the fire was just south of Greenwood, Canton, Mississippi.

11 George Raymond in Canton

NONVIOLENCE AND VIOLENCE IN CANTON

When George Raymond arrived in Canton in June 1963, he brought along his deep commitment to nonviolence. He quickly formed an alliance with local legend C. O. Chinn, but that partnership included built-in tension: Chinn always carried a gun.

And no wonder! Canton was a tough town. One freedom fighter called Canton "a hot-bed area . . . like the 'Old West.'" Raymond needed to first survive in Canton and then thrive—without resorting to violence. Apparently he found that inner strength. According to Willie Peacock, "George Raymond had guts."

Perhaps Raymond's grit grew out of his belief in nonviolence, a philosophy he developed as a member of the New Orleans chapter of CORE and then brought to Mississippi. For nonviolent activists, the strength not to fight back when attacked emerges from an inner love that seeks not to defeat attackers but rather to transform them—to consider your "enemy's" humanity and offer that person who hates and fears you the chance to see you as a human being, too. Recall that Raymond had already demonstrated his commitment to nonviolence when he traveled into McComb on a Freedom Ride and then in Jackson when he stepped into the chaos during the sit-in at Woolworth's. Canton provided Raymond another opportunity to explore and test those nonviolent principles.

As happened to Sam Block in Greenwood, when Raymond came to Canton, local people initially turned their backs. So Raymond, twenty at the time, connected with forty-four-year-old Chinn, a man who was part of Canton's old guard and who had already stood up to the White power structure. Raymond and Chinn rode together, talking to people, organizing, and becoming a team. Chinn provided Raymond a way into the community.

People in Canton knew Chinn as both a successful entrepreneur and a man you did not mess with. He owned a barroom cafe, a 152-acre farm, a bootlegging business, and "a large collection of pistols, shotguns, and rifles." While those weapons concerned Raymond, Chinn was determined to succeed in a world driven by vicious, violent racism.

CORE director Dave Dennis, who had invited Raymond to Canton, recalled that during his first visit to town for a mass meeting Chinn stood guard. Raymond, wanting to keep things nonviolent, told Dennis, "Whenever we have a meeting, C. O. Chinn sits outside with his guns. He won't leave. He says he's here to protect the people. Can you talk to him?"

When Dennis went out, he saw Chinn "sitting in the back of his truck with a shotgun across his lap and a pistol by his side." Dennis tried to explain CORE's nonviolent philosophy, but Chinn told him, "This is my town and these are my people. I'm here to protect my people and even if you don't like this I'm not going anywhere. So maybe *you* better leave." Seeing how determined Chinn was and realizing that he wasn't about to change, Dennis respectfully responded, "Yes, sir," shook Chinn's hand, and went back inside.

Despite the tension over weapons, the young activists grew to appreciate Chinn. He offered generous support, including an office at his cafe and contacts that led to church space for public meetings. Chinn and his wife Minnie told CORE activists, "If you're hungry, you come here, and you eat. If you need a place to stay, let us know. We'll get you a place to stay. If you need to go somewhere, one of us will drive you."

Over time, Raymond formed a warm relationship with Mr. and Mrs. Chinn, coming to accept and depend upon all of their support, especially because Raymond faced constant danger in Canton. And the Chinns came to respect the tenacious and non-violent Raymond, too.

George Raymond and the Campaign for Voter Registration

CORE had sent Raymond to Canton to organize a voter registration drive. The county seat of Madison County, Canton boasted a total population of 32,904, of which only 121 of 23,690 Blacks were registered to vote. Madison, shamefully similar to other Mississippi counties, needed a voter registration drive and a determined activist like Raymond to see it succeed.

In June 1963, Raymond started the registration project with a bang. During just the first three weeks of the campaign, he brought seventy-five people to the courthouse to register; twenty-five passed the test, no small feat given that Foote Campbell, the local circuit clerk who registered voters and whom one resident called "past racist," worked as hard as he could to keep African Americans from registering and voting.

When Campbell realized that someone had actually organized so Blacks could gain the vote, he fought back. He flunked some Black would-be voters because they wrote "Mr.," "Mrs.," or "Miss" in front of their names. Others, he just told to come back in a month, a year, or two years. Or Campbell simply closed his office. Some who tried to register lost their jobs as a result. Canton officials like Campbell did all they could to squash the designs of CORE and Raymond.

But the registration drive moved forward, and Raymond became a striking presence in Canton, always dressed in starched overalls and combat boots. Canton resident Jewell Williams noted, "He was so neat. He was just as neat as he wanted to be." Williams saw

Raymond in a local park passing out leaflets and was curious about his audacity, so she went up to him to ask why he was willing to put his personal safety at risk. He explained that he came from a middle-class home in New Orleans but had asked himself, "How could I be satisfied eating steak when my brothers can't even get the chitlins?" Raymond told Williams, "Until we're all free, none of us is free."

Williams admired Raymond for his courage and character: "He was a leader, very good, very forceful. . . . He was a good person too."

ANNIE DEVINE: LOCAL ACTIVIST

Though many who worked for the cause of justice were idealistic young people, seasoned adults also caught the fire of change and stepped in to move it along.

Annie Devine went by a CORE location one day and heard singing. She went in, discovered a voter registration meeting, and grew excited. She too lent her efforts to the cause.

As an insurance salesperson, Devine went door-to-door throughout Canton, combining her responsibilities as a sales representative with activism; she let people know about mass meetings and encouraged them to go register. A longtime resident and single mother of four, living most of her then fifty one years in Canton, and working at one time as an elementary school teacher, Devine's roots were deep in the community. But that did not save her from harassment. The people running the projects where she lived threatened eviction because of her activism. According to her friend Jewell Williams, "That made her mad."

Devine became a mentor for Raymond and the other youthful CORE workers, many of whom had not grown up in places such as Canton. One acknowledged, "We understood very little about Mississippi and how Whites and Blacks related to each other," but Devine "knew her community and understood it. . . . She directed us to Blacks who were trustworthy, to ministers and churches that would open, and [told us] how to approach these people. . . . She was a stabilizing force . . . the backbone of what we were doing." Initially, as in other places, many ministers feared the repercussions of getting involved with the movement, but Devine provided a force that shamed some into opening up their churches to the cause.

Much of Devine's impact came from her thoughtful nature. One interviewer described her as "deliberate and meditative," adding that she possessed a "power of reflection and quality of analysis."

Eventually, Devine quit her job selling insurance to become a full-time movement leader, running the CORE office.

Where C. O. Chinn represented the more idiosyncratic, outlaw elements of Canton, Annie Devine spoke for the professional classes. Raymond needed both types to create an inclusive movement. As adults became involved, moving into leadership positions, they were bound to notice that Canton's children had already laid a foundation on which to build.

ANNE MOODY ORGANIZES THE YOUNG PEOPLE

In early summer of 1963, reinforcements showed up in Canton. Anne Moody, a student from nearby Tougaloo College and a veteran of the Woolworth's sit-in, moved into town. Her first night in Canton she dined with Raymond and others and then settled into the Freedom House, a former residence that served as a local movement headquarters as well as a home for the out-of-town activists.

As Moody began her work, she focused on Canton's teens, a group crucial to the success of the voter registration drive. According to one historian, "But here again young people served as the shock troops of the movement." Every day fifty young people headed to the CORE office and then out into the streets. Their canvassing invited older people to come down to the courthouse to register.

Soon, of course, a backlash turned Canton nasty. After a rally on July 24, five young people walked down Pear Street past a gas station owned by Price Lewis, a White man. According to Moody, who heard the story from the teens,

> Then just as they were crossing the railroad tracks to the left of the service station, they heard a loud noise. They looked back and noticed that Price Lewis was now holding a shotgun pointed in their direction. At this point, one of the girls said she looked down and discovered blood was running down her legs into her shoes. She realized she had been shot and saw that the others had been wounded by buckshot pellets too.

The shotgun blast sent them to the hospital; all survived. Police arrested and jailed Lewis but released him in an hour after he posted bail. The court eventually fined Lewis five hundred dollars for "unlawful discharge of a firearm within the city limits . . ." Temporarily, young people stopped flocking to the CORE office. The parents, rightfully, became scared for their children.

But the fear did not last.

To draw teens back and energize them, Moody held Saturday night parties at the CORE office. The young people came and sang freedom songs. One week, she visited the Black high school to let the kids know about the upcoming party. Even though the principal banned Moody from the school grounds and warned his students they would be expelled if they attended, the party had a huge turnout.

Then Moody's young recruits started to act independently. Moody watched one Monday as her charges left school and hosted their own rally behind the Boyd Street housing projects. She was thrilled to see their initiative! "I wanted badly to attend it, but I knew the teenagers had to make their own decisions." After the rally, the teens marched into the projects, "singing freedom songs, with the chief and two carloads of police driving alongside them."

Moody had paid attention to the young people and harnessed their energy. As in so many other towns, the kids played a central role in Canton's drive for social justice.

WHITE BACKLASH AND SOME RESPONSE

That fall and winter, harassment from Canton's White power structure escalated.

Police showed up at meetings, taking down the names and addresses of attendees and following people home. One result of that surveillance: some people lost their jobs.

And authorities who had earlier displayed tolerance got tough with Chinn as he pushed harder for civil rights. Officials took away Chinn's liquor license, forcing him to close his bar. But Chinn continued in his civil rights activities. One day when police stopped his pickup, they noticed a gun on the seat, arrested him, and charged him with carrying a concealed weapon. Chinn spent six months in jail.

Raymond also remained vulnerable. At a meeting in late January where Raymond spoke, someone overheard one city detective threaten, "I'm going to kill a nigger tonight." That evening the highway patrol and a posse of eight cars followed Raymond and, according to a CORE report, he

> was taken behind the patrol car and found Constable Herbie Evans waiting there. Evans challenged Raymond to a fist fight and removed his badge, gun and watch and verbally taunted him to fight. When Raymond remained passive, Evans kicked him several times, knocking him against the back of the patrol car. Evans then let him go.

That harassment seemed only to spur the people on. In early 1964, CORE added a new tactic to their voter registration drive:

they boycotted local stores. A mimeographed flyer announced, "Don't Buy at These Stores" and then presented the names of sixteen merchants being targeted for their policies. CORE laid out its demands: treat Blacks courteously when they come into stores and hire more Blacks to work in the stores. The boycott also pressured Foote Campbell to register more Black voters. During the boycott, 90 per cent of the African Americans in Canton stopped shopping at the stores on the list.

More was happening. Around two hundred people were turning up for the weekly two mass meetings. And the teens had come back. Young people continued to canvass the town and speak in churches.

Seeing that activist Black community, Whites in Canton reorganized their White Citizens' Council. Its steering committee included the mayor, law enforcement, and businesspeople. The *New York Times* reported that "virtually every business establishment has a Council sticker on its door or in its front window." The merchants didn't have much choice. The WCC applied pressure, threatening a *White* boycott of stores that did not comply with their demand to join the segregationist organization.

Violence continued to escalate. Racists bombed homes, churches, stores, and offices. They bombed Pleasant Green Holiness Church where mass meetings were held, the Freedom House, and George Washington's store across the street from the Freedom House because Washington owned its building.

The backlash against the voter registration drive and boycott was well-organized, determined, and mean. But, despite that brutality from the White power structure and its supporters, CORE kept up the fight.

FREEDOM DAYS

In early 1964, CORE held three "Freedom Days" to energize the voter registration campaign. They announced in a flyer:

Citizens of Madison County, February 28, 1964, is the day when everyone should be at the courthouse in unity, to express to everyone that Negroes do and will vote in Madison County. . . . We will be there to help you register to vote.

Police got the message, and on that first Freedom Day they arrived in droves. According to one observer, "as we neared the courthouse, helmeted police with guns were everywhere in evidence."

Despite that forceful presence, three hundred and fifty people, many elderly, arrived at the courthouse that Friday. Showing no respect for age, "city policemen armed with nightsticks, revolvers and a variety of shotguns and rifles snapped orders at the Negroes as they shepherded them through a crosswalk to the courthouse grounds," the *Times* reported.

The would-be registrants stood outside the 1857 brick, white-columned courthouse, "some wrinkled and bent with age" and they "waited patiently." As they waited "a sheriff's deputy . . . paced up and down the lines, an automatic carbine swinging in his left hand and a wooden club dangling from his belt." Two police dogs and fire-fighting equipment stood at the ready.

Deputy Sheriff Billy Noble approached each person in line and barked, "What is your business here?" To which people standing in line responded, "To register." Noble then demanded, "Are you a resident of Madison County?" and people responded, "Yes, born and raised here."

The lawmen permitted one person into the courthouse at a time, and the registrar dawdled with each individual. In fact, only five managed to register that Friday. Greeting those few who were admitted to Campbell's office was a Confederate flag hanging on the wall, and a sign on the window that read, "Support Your Citizens' Council." Foote Campbell wished to make his views crystal clear. One lucky woman who actually got inside the office during a March

People in Canton heading to the courthouse to register for voting. Two policemen stand guard holding rifles and carrying tear gas equipment.

Freedom Day described her experience, providing an explanation for why the process took so long:

> I actually stood outside the courthouse for an hour before I was permitted to enter. I was only about the second person in line. When I was told that I could enter, I found that I had to stand in the corridor for another half an hour. . . . After that, the registrar came out of his office and went to lunch and I was told to go back outside to wait for him to return.
>
> After another hour, he came back from lunch, and I was told to come into the office. It took me about fifteen minutes to fill out the application. The registrar said that it would be about thirty days before I would be able to know if I had passed or not.

That day, the people stood in line for five and a half hours.

At an impromptu press conference, Raymond announced, "Today's activities disprove previous statements made by state and local officials that a large assembly of Negroes would create violence."

A victory followed. The U.S. Justice Department sued Foote Campbell, stating that his registration procedures discriminated against Blacks in Madison County by using different standards and procedures for Blacks and Whites. A federal judge ordered Campbell to process at least fifty applicants a day.

The African Americans of Canton kept up the pressure. Two more Freedom Days took place on March 13 and May 29.

School Boycott

Young people plotted as well. In the midst of the Freedom Day activities, Canton's Black students called for a boycott of their Jim Crow schools. They had grown tired, maybe sickened, of the conditions within those schools, especially when compared to the White counterparts.

One Sunday the students sent their list of concerns to the superintendent of schools and to Mayor Stanley Matthews, a list that included the following:

- books in poor repair and not enough of them,
- not enough chemicals and equipment for the chemistry laboratory,
- no foreign languages taught,
- insufficient first aid equipment,
- insufficient library,
- inadequate shop facilities,
- overcrowded and broken buses,
- no lockers for students
- overcrowded classes,

• building in poor repair.

The next day, Monday, March 2, six hundred and twenty-five students from Rogers Junior-Senior High and from Cameron Street Elementary didn't show up at school. Instead, one hundred and fifteen attended a "Freedom School" at Pleasant Green Holiness Church, studying inequality in a Jim Crow school system and nonviolence.

Anne Moody's push to make young people more independent must have been paying off. As one CORE report acknowledged, students had "organized the boycott almost completely by themselves."

Later that afternoon, as students left their freedom school two-by-two, they encountered "five squad cars, policemen standing in the road armed with shotguns and rifles." Officials feared any action that threatened the town's racial status quo. They acted against anyone they viewed as agitators, including the young. But one observer noted that the police were "helpless before children who, led by a great idea, walked this bristling gauntlet apparently unafraid."

THE CANTON FREEDOM MOVEMENT

The struggle for civil rights and equality in Canton mirrored the struggle throughout the state. Led by freedom fighters such as George Raymond, Annie Devine, C. O. Chinn, and Anne Moody, the citizens of Canton organized and fought for the vote and a more just society. The fight in Canton became a community affair, driven by some older local leaders and a youthful CORE leadership, but galvanized by a vital cadre of young people.

The mass meetings continued and sustained the spirit of the cause. At a Pleasant Green Holiness Church mass meeting, "the people sang, clapped their hands and rejoiced" even as "White citizens in pickup trucks and squad cars repeatedly circled the church peering through the windows." Activity continued through the spring of 1964, all in the face of relentless and spiteful response from Whites and White authorities.

And then came Freedom Summer. White officials ran even more scared.

In a letter to members of the White Citizens' Council, Gus Noble let Whites know what was at stake by that campaign to register as many African American voters as possible:

> Outside groups have promised to bring thousands of agitators to our state this summer. Canton is one of the 25 towns listed by the agitators as demonstration centers. THE WHITE CITIZENS OF CANTON MUST BE UNIFIED TO SAVE CANTON FROM MASS CONFUSION LEADING TO RACE MIXING. . . .

But the boycott of stores went on, and people continued their marches to the courthouse, demanding the vote. With Raymond still active and young people still committed, new faces and ten freedom schools would be coming to Madison County.

12 Freedom Summer, Freedom Schools, a Legacy of Activism

As they tried to design and build a movement to end decades of entrenched injustice, SNCC members often clashed forcefully with each other. They were fighting so hard and under such threat, it is no wonder that internal disagreements were passionate and members' opinions tied closely to their heartfelt beliefs. So when some advocated bringing outsiders—meaning mainly White students from the North—to help support the Mississippi movement, angry opposition arose.

Those disagreeing with the plan argued that bringing in non-native activists violated everything SNCC stood for, especially the idea that *local* people should run the show and lead the fight for justice within their own towns. The critics did not see the need for a cavalry of White kids riding in and taking over the campaigns that they and people from the community had worked so hard to create and nurture.

Proponents countered that new blood, White or Black, could energize the ongoing struggle. Further, they reminded their comrades that White people up North shamefully paid little attention when Black people got killed or abused in the South, especially when those harmed were people speaking up, fighting for rights. Maybe if Mississippi racists assaulted Northern college kids, someone would take notice. As an added bonus, if White kids came to the state, the federal government might be more ready to protect everyone, including the Black activists already on the ground.

The discussion grew in intensity; eventually, the pro side won out.

In the summer of 1964 COFO (Council of Federated Organizations) brought more than one thousand volunteers from the North into Mississippi. Most were White and most were college students. The campaign was initially called the "Summer Project"; it became known, fittingly, as "Freedom Summer."

Some of those volunteers organized and ran what was perhaps the most amazing invention of Freedom Summer—Freedom Schools.

CHARLIE COBB AND THE FREEDOM SCHOOL IDEA

The Mississippi school system was rotten for Whites and even worse for Blacks. Recall the deplorable school conditions laid out by the students in Canton during their boycott. Beyond the inadequate facilities and weak curricula, Mississippi schools did not teach Black history or literature, effectively saying to Black kids that African Americans had no history, had created no literature, were not really an important part of the nation or world, and had done little of importance. At that time, Mississippi's public school officials allotted four times as much funding for White students as they did for Black students. Teachers in the resulting separate-but-unequal schools generally taught students to accept things as they were and not to question the arrangement; it made no difference to the State of Mississippi that what students learned to accept was a Jim Crow world, monstrous and mean.

SNCC field secretary Charlie Cobb was sickened by those educational realities and envisioned a new kind of school— a "Freedom School." Cobb pushed the idea as a project for Freedom Summer, wishing to counter the damage done to Black kids by the Mississippi school system. Others listened, and in the spring

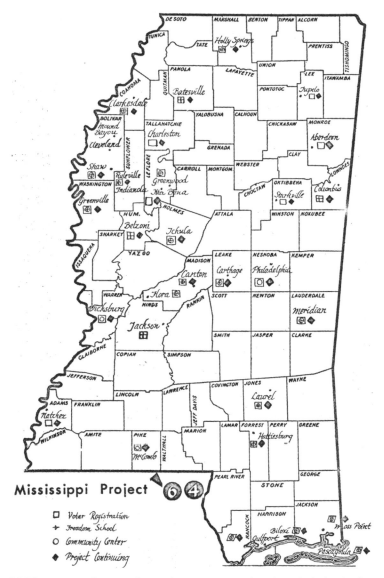

COFO-prepared map of Freedom Summer sites in Mississippi of freedom schools, voter registration projects, community centers, and areas slated for continuing projects after the 1964 summer project was over.

of 1964 a two-day conference met in New York City to create a Freedom School blueprint.

The conference organizers designed schools grounded in the reality Mississippi kids faced. They wanted to give the students the chance to examine that reality, ask some hard questions, and then form a new vision that challenged the Mississippi status quo and moved the young people toward activism on their own behalf. Organizers said: "The Freedom School idea is to train and educate people to be active agents in bringing about social change." Empowerment!

GETTING THE SCHOOLS UP AND RUNNING

Before heading to Mississippi, all Freedom Summer volunteers attended an orientation in Oxford, Ohio. Each received an assignment for the summer, some working for voter registration, others for the Mississippi Freedom Democratic Party, and still others as teachers in the Freedom Schools that opened in early July 1964.

No one knew if these experimental schools would even get off the ground. Teachers had to create the schools from scratch, first recruiting their students, a task made difficult because so many of the young people had to work.

But in getting their students, the teachers did have one thing going for them: the new visitors caused a stir in the small rural communities and even in larger cities, and everyone was curious about the strangers—those college kids from the North. The volunteers used that attention to advertise the schools. The teachers also visited churches, trailed along with canvassers for voter registration, and talked up the Freedom Schools as they moved through the community. Sometimes they met potential students who were hanging out in freedom houses.

Freedom Schools met in churches, homes, lodge halls, storefronts, college campuses, out of doors—almost anyplace.

One teacher in Canton described the trials of recruiting a class. The volunteers cleaned up the church where the school was to be held, but "on registration day nobody came." So they "combed the area for students," finding out that "some were holding back out of fear—their own and/or their parents' (this building was bombed a month ago; the police have been circling it almost hourly since we moved into it)." Teachers discovered that "many distrusted us; some simply didn't care." Somehow, things worked out. According to the teacher, ". . . by some mysterious force. . . . a few people began appearing for classes, averaging about twenty a day now—never the same twenty."

All of that early work paid off better than expected. Organizers had hoped to educate one thousand students, mainly at the high school level. In actuality, forty-one schools across the state served more than three thousand students during the summer of 1964. Numbers swelled as elementary-aged kids appeared, as well as older adults; teachers accommodated everyone who showed up.

INSIDE THE CLASSES

As with all teaching, some Freedom School classes seemed to fall flat while others bubbled. Pam Parker's (later Chude Pamela Allen) experience rose to the up side. As she said in a letter home to Pennsylvania, "The atmosphere in class is unbelievable. It is what every teacher dreams about—real, honest enthusiasm and desire to learn anything and everything. The girls come to class of their own free will. They respond to everything that is said. They are excited about learning."

Teachers maintained informal classrooms in the Freedom Schools. Students sat where they wished, often in circles. They called the teachers by their first names. If someone needed to go to the bathroom, they just went—no need to raise your hand and obtain permission. Teachers learned to be very flexible.

That atmosphere enabled teachers to build a safe and comfortable space that encouraged students to share thoughts and feelings about their lives. As Jackson teacher Florence Howe described, "In your 'class,' your teacher sat with you in a circle, and soon you got the idea that you could say what you thought and that no one, least of all the teacher, would laugh at you or strike you . . . that your teacher was really interested in what *you* thought or felt."

Naturally, questioning and discussion became the favored teaching methods. Teachers asked thought-provoking questions like, "What do we mean when we say 'Things are bad in Mississippi?'" and "What do White people have that we want?" "What do they have that we don't want?" One teacher had students explore the question of school integration, asking the students if Black schools and White schools were equal "would they still favor integrated schools?" The teacher concluded the lesson by asking students if they thought "Negroes and Whites in Mississippi really understood each other?"

Whole lessons were built on the model of inquiry. For instance, Howe encouraged students to explore and discuss a real situation: Local ministers, pushing to integrate local elementary schools, called a prayer meeting to encourage parents to enroll their kids in an all-White elementary school. Apparently, interest in the meeting was low. So Howe invited her students to discuss this call from the ministers and to explain why parents seemed reluctant to attend the meeting.

Initially, students provided only superficial answers, prompting Howe to energize the conversation by asking, "What am I going to say to my friends back North when they ask me why Negro mothers haven't registered children in White schools? That they like things the way they are?" That question shook the students, and they "then began to explore their real feelings and fears. Jobs might be lost, personal safety was threatened, and possible failure in White

In a Freedom School in Indianola in the summer of 1964, students learning in an outdoor classroom.

schools loomed high." The talk then moved toward activism. One of the students suggested they go out into the community, speak with the parents of first-graders, and encourage them to attend the meeting. Others readily agreed. The students then prepared for their outreach by role-playing the conversation they would have with the parents.

On Monday and Tuesday of the next week, the students headed out into the community and spoke with seventy families, explaining why the moms and dads should attend the meeting and hear more about the push for integration. The students eventually convinced eleven of the parents to come, one more step toward integration. In the spirit of the Freedom School idea, students moved from inquiry to action.

Then there was the content studied. In the Freedom School classrooms, students often explored Black history and Black litera-ture—topics they never encountered in their regular schools, topics that even students in the North rarely encountered at that time. As one volunteer writing home about segregated Blacks schools stated, "They learn nothing of the contributions Negroes have made to our culture or anything else which would give them any reason to disbelieve the lies they are told about Negroes being unable to do anything worthwhile."

In their training, teachers received the curriculum package, *Guide to Negro History*, which took the students through a series of topics from a study of African Americans at the founding of the republic, to an examination of active forms of resistance as the nation rolled toward Civil War, to a discussion of Reconstruction and the movement toward a Jim Crow system, and finally to a consideration of Black life from 1890 into the new century and up to the present. This curriculum became the foundation for studying Black history in the Freedom Schools.

In literature, students studied African American writers such as Langston Hughes, Richard Wright, James Baldwin, and Frederick Douglass. The poet Hughes seemed to be particularly popular. As Howe noted, "The students who had never heard of Langston Hughes were surprised by his slang, by his use of jazz expressions." Howe's students then went on to write their own poems in their own voices.

Students read and even saw plays with Black history themes such as *In White America* by Princeton professor Martin Duberman that examines how racism affected both Blacks and Whites from colonial times to *Brown v. Board of Education*.

Through the Citizenship curriculum, students explored social and political issues they might actually face: what life in the North was like and how it differed or not from their own in the South; how poor Whites and poor Blacks were different but the same; the power structure; the movement; and so on.

Students also studied more traditional subjects such as math and science, but in addition the Freedom Schools offered literacy classes for adults so they could register to vote, foreign languages for kids in high schools where such instruction did not exist, religion, and more.

Teachers in the Freedom Schools used the Afro-rich and issue-oriented curricula they were given, combining it with the liberating atmosphere they created. Together, these pushed the students to find themselves in history and literature as teachers personalized the subjects in ways students had never experienced, connecting what they learned to their world and gaining self-understanding and a new way to think about world problems. As part of the process, as students observed and reflected on the issues in their lives, they developed ways to express what was in their heads and in their hearts. They took to paper—writing—and honed their voices for others to hear.

Student Expression, Student Voice: Poems and Newspapers

Teachers found many ways to help students convey their thoughts and emotions in writing, encouraging each student to share those ideas and feelings in his or her unique manner—in other words, through his or her "voice." Educator Tom Romano called voice "the writer's presence in a piece of writing." I am certain you will feel the presence of the young writers in the sample pieces presented below.

For Freedom School students, voice came through the poetry they wrote, poetry that presented observations, emotional reactions, and strong opinions about their lives in Mississippi. Fifteen-year-old Edith Moore, writing about conditions in McComb, included all three in her poem, "Isn't it Awful":

> Isn't it awful not to be able to eat in a public place
> Without being arrested or snarled at right in your face?
> Isn't it awful not to be able to go to a public library

and get an interesting book
Without being put out and given a hateful look?
Isn't it awful not to be able to sleep peacefully nights
For fear you may get bombed because you want your rights?
Isn't it awful not to be able to get your schooling where you please?
Just because of our race, color and creed we cannot feel at ease.

Some poetry laid out the conditions poets wanted to change, as captured by these lines in Allen Goodner's poem:

Segregation will not be here long.
I will do my best to see it gone.

Other students used their writing for self-exploration. Sandra Jo-Ann O. from Hattiesburg wrote "Who Am I?":

Who am I, let me see,
Am I a dog or am I a bee?
Am I a maniac who's out of her mind?
I think I know and I'll tell you
I'm not the girl I used to be. . . .
Who am I? I have to know
So I may tell it wherever I go
I'll tell it to men of all the land,
I'll tell it to kids who shake my hand,
That I am free and it shows
To everyone over all the land.
Who am I? I'll tell you now,
I'll have to find words, but I'll tell it somehow.
I am a Negro who fought her best
To earn her freedom and deserves to rest
So do as I did, and you'll be free,

Just don't hit back, and you'll win
Your rest.

In a Biloxi Freedom School, a twelve-year-old girl turned in "What is Wrong," crying in her sister's arms after she gave it to her teacher:

What is wrong with me everywhere I go
No one seems to look at me
Sometimes I cry.
I walk through the woods and sit on a stone.
I look at the stars and I sometimes wish.
Probably if my wish ever comes true,
Everybody will look at me.

Journalist Len Holt, observing twelve-year-old Ida Ruth Griffin reading her poem, commented, "Her eyes sparkled with a deep fire as her voice came forth melodiously and with just a dramatic tinge; she read in a slow cadence":

I am Mississippi-fed,
I am Mississippi-bred,
Nothing but a poor, Black boy.
I am a Mississippi slave,
I shall be buried in a Mississippi grave,
Nothing but a poor, dead boy.

The poem troubled the students and a discussion ensued. Holt continued, "In an angry chorus they responded with fierce refutations: 'We're not Black slaves!' The teacher didn't know what to do, but he waited for the talk to move forward. 'She's right,' spoke another student, a tall reedy girl with a sharp mind. 'We certainly are. Can your poppa vote? Can mine? Can our folks eat anywhere they want to?' And this led to a cacophony of talking and thinking aloud, scattering ideas."

And then there were the newspapers with names like the *Freedom Star, Benton County Freedom Train,* and *Freedom's Journal.* Students produced them in their schools and distributed them through churches, grocery stores, and restaurants. Giving the young people a platform where they could state their views publicly and push hard for change allowed them to join that great American tradition of written protest and transformed them into activists.

Take for example this article, "Why I Deserve Freedom," by fifteen-year-old Albert J. Evans:

> I am a Negro, I am a Black man. And because of my color, I am deprived of the human rights which are given to me by God and promised to me by the United States. I live in a country of free people, yet I am not free.
>
> The Bill of Rights guarantees to everyone the freedoms of religion, and the rights of peaceful assembly, but in Mississippi these rights are denied to Negroes. The 13 Amendment abolished slavery. I deserve freedom because the law of the land states this.
>
> The Negroes of the past have fought for freedom inside and outside the United States. Crispus Attucks, a man of Negro blood, was the first to be killed in the struggle to free our great nation from its mother country. He was described by Poet John Boyle O'Reilly as "the first to defy and the first to die." Thus history has recorded that I have a stake in freedom.
>
> If necessary, I will die in order to have freedom for my children.
>
> Today I am the world's footstool but tomorrow I hope to be one of its leaders. By attending freedom school this summer I am preparing for that tomorrow.

Student writing in the various newspapers touched on topics including Black history, life in the segregated South, activism, and the theme of freedom. They included news stories, political essays, poetry, and opinion pieces.

Twelve of the forty-one Freedom Schools produced newspapers, each unique. For instance, *The Student Voice of Truelight*, created in 1964 by the students at a Hattiesburg Freedom School, was six pages long and contained one article on segregation in Hattiesburg, another on slavery, a third that explored what the word *freedom* meant, and interviews with girls who tested the new civil rights act by sitting at lunch counters.

Classrooms where young people produced their own newspapers hummed. Students generally took over the operation, writing articles on donated typewriters and printing editions on donated mimeograph machines. A teacher in Clarksdale described one classroom engaged in such a journalistic venture: "The place looked just like a newspaper office with people running in and out, with typewriters going, and newsprint everywhere. It was excellent experience for the kids too. . . . They did most of the work and made most of the decisions." As with the poetry, students shared their careful observations and their blunt feelings about what they experienced in Jim Crow Mississippi. Once again, students found their voices and used them in their writing.

Here, for instance, is a whimsical letter from *The Student Voice of Truelight* written by thirteen-year-old Shelly S.:

Dear President Johnson,

We are in the 8 and 9 grade class of Freedom School in the state of Mississippi. We are measuring the distance around the tops of our Freedom Schools. We use our own spirit as the unit of measurement. Since the President is the most important person in our country, we decided we would use your spirit so as to make us free from slavery. We will call it a "Johnson" and measure our Freedom Schools in "Johnsons."

We know you are a busy man, but could you send us your own freedom measurement?

Yours truly,

Shelley S., age 13

We don't know if President Johnson responded.

A few writers celebrated their own activism. In "When I Was Going on Hardy Street," ten-year-old Mattie Jean Wilson shared her experience on a bus:

Well, it was this bus driver. I was on the first straight seat on the bus, and he told me to move back. I said, "I will not. I paid a dime and two pennies for a transfer and I'm not moving." He said, "You know White people must get on this bus." I said, "You know Colored people must get on this bus, too."

Mattie M. in Hattiesburg wrote an article entitled, "What the Summer Has Meant to Me":

I think this summer has made a lot of changes in Mississippi. Now we can sit down and eat at Woolworth's and Kress.

I think the summer has made the White man see that we are not happy with Mississippi. We want to make even more changes.

I think the next summer we can get to go to more than just two places in Hattiesburg. We should be able to go to the drive-in.

Some students saved the greatest anger for their own experiences within the local schools. In a *Palmer's Crossing Freedom News* piece, "The Darkness of the Negro Students," Linda C. critiqued how she had been taught Black history:

Some of the Negro students have been complaining about their teachers. They said their teachers do not give any information about the freeing of their people. The information given to them was false. They teach only what the White man wants us to hear. We have been taught that the White man was responsible for the abolishing of slavery, but that is false. What about the Negro abolitionists?

We have been taught that when Negroes were free, they were helpless. But this is false because they helped themselves by building houses and raising crops.

The reason for my coming out of the darkness is by attending Freedom Schools. At this school both sides of the story are told.

You might notice that articles do not often include the author's last names. Such anonymity was necessary, given that many of the students writing in the Freedom School newspapers were attacking the Jim Crow system that Whites were fighting tooth and nail to maintain. The young journalists knew that many White people were threatened by what they were writing and might very well harm them or their families.

For Black kids growing up in the Jim Crow South, kids who received a message at school and on the street that maybe they weren't worth much, or at least not as much as White kids, it is amazing that when given the opportunity those same kids burst out their thinking and emotions with such honesty and beauty. Their poems and newspaper articles represented a frontal assault on the forces driving Jim Crow. We are fortunate to still have these creations that allow us to see into the heads and hearts of the young people in Mississippi during the excitement and turmoil of Freedom Summer.

ACTIVISM

In addition to their educational and creative aspects, the Freedom Schools led to some direct student activism, too, both in

1964 and later. For instance, Freedom School students canvassed neighborhoods for people to register to vote. Teacher Sandra Adickes described one young person, Rita Mae Crawford, as "the best canvasser among us" and said, "I enjoyed watching her approach adults, who were at first patronizingly amused by her question, 'Have you went to register?' but quickly became defensive when she refused to accept their excuses and persistently demanded that they register to vote."

Eddie James Carthan, another Freedom School student, felt "canvassing was tough work. . . . We'd have certain days we'd go out and canvass all day." Anthony Harris remembered "having doors slammed in our faces and people being angry with us for knocking on their doors" and that "people were afraid. They were very much afraid to talk to us."

Beyond the good work they did, the students gained invaluable lessons. Canvassing in the Delta, Carthan came face-to-face with a bleak Delta poverty he had never seen before. As he said, "It was quite an experience to see how my folk were living and suffering, but through it all they survived." The students went door-to-door, as well as onto plantations, talking to people in the community, encouraging them to register or to come out and attend mass meetings, gaining a profound education in real life through their activism.

As the McGhee brothers did in Greenwood, students all over tested the new Civil Rights Act of 1964.

Perhaps in imitation of the Tougaloo Nine, Adickes and six of her Hattiesburg students visited the local library where they approached a young woman sitting at a desk and asked for library cards. Adickes reported that the clerk's eyes "nearly bolted" from their sockets.

The young woman called a librarian who lectured the students about "a custom that has been here since you were born" and explained that the "Council had decreed that the library not be integrated." According to Adickes, "The students listened patiently and then replied that they could not see why they should not have library cards. The librarian continued talking at some length as the students continued to listen patiently." When students did try to talk, the librarian said—with no awareness of irony, apparently— "Look, close your mouths and open your minds."' Finally the librarian told the students that if they stayed she would call the police. Adickes asked the students what they wanted to do; they told her they wanted to stay. The young activists found some soft chairs, sat down, and read newspapers. Soon the police arrived and shut down the library. Adickes stated, "I was very impressed by the students' demeanor; throughout the encounter, they had been dignified and courteous but determined."

After the students and their teacher left the library, they went down to the Kress department store to celebrate, to eat, and maybe to cause a little more "good trouble," in John Lewis's phrase. The waitress took orders from the students, but not Adickes. The waitress told the White teacher, "We're not going to serve you. We have to serve the Colored, but we're not serving the Whites who come in with them." Everyone in the group got up and left. As they walked down the street, the police arrested Adickes for vagrancy, even though she had seventy dollars in her pocket.

To bolster the activist spirit, Freedom Summer culminated in a convention. The Mississippi Student Union (MSU), an organization set up as a mechanism for coordinating the civil rights activities of young people throughout the state, held its convention in Meridian August 6–8, 1964, with each member school sending three representatives, for a total of one hundred and twenty delegates. The convention goal was to formulate a youth plan for the Mississippi Freedom Democratic Party that was challenging the seating of the all-White Mississippi Democratic Party delegation at the upcoming Democratic National Convention in Atlantic City, New Jersey. In

Young students singing freedom songs and clapping at a Freedom School convention in Meridian.

a setting where they took charge, the young people laid out and passed a suggested platform for the adults.

Over the next year, student activism fueled by the spirit of Freedom Schools continued. When students who had attended Freedom Schools returned to their regular schools, they showed their teachers, principals, and fellow students a new spirit that led to new actions: organizing and petitioning the administration to change or improve fundamental aspects of the public schools (Liberty, Mississippi); wearing their SNCC "One Man, One Vote" buttons to school (Philadelphia, Mississippi); staging an eight-month boycott when they were forbidden to wear their SNCC buttons (Issaquena and Sharkey counties); boycotting schools; demanding improvement in schools (Bolivar County); and picketing in front of the courthouse for voter rights and getting arrested (Cleveland, Mississippi).

Freedom School students remained active in their communities. Some were at the forefront of efforts to desegregate Mississippi public schools in 1965, and many were among the first Black students to enroll in previously all-White high schools.

Throughout the fall of 1964, Freedom School alumni took part in activities to desegregate public facilities in their communities, continuing to push enforcement of the Civil Rights Act of 1964. For instance, Eddie Carthan integrated a barber shop in the Delta. Wilbur Colom helped desegregate many places in Ripley, Mississippi, including Renfrow's Cafe, the local swimming pool, and the Dixie Theatre. He recalled, "We went downstairs and we sat down and White people threw popcorn and soda at us as we tried to watch the movie." Colom's actions led him to jail, but Freedom School alumni stood at the center of civil rights activities, working to desegregate facilities in other Mississippi towns, that summer of 1964 and in the years that followed.

FREEDOM SCHOOLS AND FREEDOM SUMMER—TODAY

Many students who attended Freedom Schools reported that activism remained a part of their lives as they moved into adulthood. Homer Hill, a Freedom School student from Clarksdale, stated in a recent interview, "It wasn't until much later that I appreciated how important those schools were . . . I carry that experience to this very day . . . [attending the Freedom School] was like shining a very bright light into a very dark place for a time and it just changed my perception about many things for the rest of my life."

And Freedom Schools themselves remain. Today the Children's Defense Fund (CDF) sponsors Freedom Schools every summer and over the course of the school year. In 2019, Freedom Schools existed in ninety-seven cities and served 12,138 students. The goals remain the same as the Freedom Schools of the sixties, as stated on the CDF website: "Through the CDF Freedom Schools model, we empower youth to excel and believe in their ability to make a difference in themselves, their families, communities, country and world with hope, education and action."

The spirit and practices of Freedom Schools continue.

As the Narrative Draws to a Close

Freedom Summer took place just nine years after the lynching of Emmett Till. Some of the older Freedom School students might have heard about what happened to Emmett at the time of the murder; others likely found out through stories told by older members of the community. Emmett's murder hovered like a dark cloud over the schools, over Freedom Summer, over the entire Mississippi Freedom Struggle. In the pieces written by the students and the activists during Freedom Summer, we see a firm rejection of the Jim Crow world that allowed Emmett's murder and an affirmation in the calls for a different world, a much better one.

I see something heroic in the ability of young people to envision a new world and then to act, even when they are living within a world that pushes them to remain passive and doubtful, a world that sends a message that they are not worth much and can do little of any value, let alone change the world around them. As I said before, we often look to grand figures in history, people like Martin Luther King Jr. and Abraham Lincoln, for our inspiration, but now I hope you see we also need to look beyond adults, beyond the well known leaders, to grasp how things change. We need to look behind the historical curtains to discover people like the children of Mississippi, the ones who were a part of the Mississippi Freedom Struggle, the ones who said "One Day!"—and then acted to show everyone a better way to live.

The children of the Mississippi Freedom Struggle helped to

create a world that was different from the past—and better. Recall how young activists sat in libraries and movie theaters and department store lunch counters to show, in a simple but unmistakable way, what a just world might look like.

Politically, that world began with the Civil Rights Act of 1964. Then came the Voting Rights Act of 1965 that opened the right to vote to people who had been denied the ballot. Recall how young activists canvassed door-to-door and marched to courthouses throughout Mississippi to show the nation that American democracy was not living up to its promise, that African Americans had been denied a fundamental democratic right.

And as the children gained a sense of empowerment, they changed the world and changed how they saw themselves. In fact, perhaps the deepest changes took place inside each person who refused to see himself or herself as anything less than a human being with dignity.

We need to take a troubling step back. As with the children of Mississippi, the murder of Emmett Till and the ugly world the murder took place in continue to haunt us. There is a historical marker outside the derelict hulk of what was once Bryant's Grocery. In April 2017, someone defaced the marker, erasing the photos and text that explained what had happened at the store and what happened to Emmett. That was the second time the marker was vandalized, and by then someone had already shot up the sign marking the site along the Tallahatchie River where Emmett's body was found. The marker by the store was repaired. In October 2019, a fourth sign officially replaced the earlier ones that had stood by the river. The new one is made of bulletproof steel. Clearly, some are determined to erase the memory of Emmett Till, but others are determined to see that never happens.

Telling and remembering are important. The newly built National Museum of African American History and Culture offers profound help. Emmett Till's casket is solemnly displayed at the museum, helping to keep alive the memory of Emmett's murder and Mamie Till-Mobley's brave actions. Other parts of the museum help visitors learn about how the Emmett Till generation—the children talked about in this book—let that memory move them to act.

And how do these freedom fighters connect to you? Do you see anything personal, anything about yourself when you encounter people like the Tougaloo Nine, Brenda Travis, Luvaughn Brown, June Johnson, and all the young people talked about throughout this book? Are there places in your lives, your schools, or your communities where you see injustice or oppression? Do the adults and those with power hear your voices? Do they try to keep you in "your place"? Or, as Freedom School students were prompted to do, are you encouraged to examine your world and then consider ways you and your peers might act to make the world better?

Some historians argue that the civil rights movement never ended, that issues driving the movement remain, as do people acting in the spirit of the earlier freedom fighters. For instance, today we continue to experience the disregard for Black lives in the form of killings, both by police and others, reminding us that wrongful deaths like Emmett Till's still occur. We can see hope in the rising of the Black Lives Matter (BLM) movement as well as of organizations working to stop all forms of racism. As in Mississippi in the 1960s, young people stand at the center of today's fight to protect and honor Black lives.

So the civil rights movement is ongoing. I'm wondering if you agree. If so, one thing we can do is not let vandals blot out our history. And we can all capture the spirit of people like Sam Block and the Ladner sisters and continue the battle they began. There is, in truth, still much to be done. Much to be done.

Sources of Illustrations

· ·

Bibliography

Adickes, Sandra E. *The Legacy of a Freedom School*. New York: Palgrave Macmillan, 2005.

Anderson, Devery S. *Emmett Till: The Murder That Shocked the World and Propelled the Civil Rights Movement*. Jackson: University Press of Mississippi, 2015.

Arsenault, Raymond. *Freedom Riders: 1961 and the Struggle for Racial Justice*. New York: Oxford University Press, 2006.

"The Battle of Jackson." *Newsweek*, June 10, 1963.

Booker, Simeon. *Shocking the Conscience: A Reporter's Account of the Civil Rights Movement*. Jackson: University Press of Mississippi, 2013.

Branch, Taylor. *Parting the Waters: America in the King Years 1954–63*. New York: Simon & Schuster, 1988.

Burner, Eric. *And Gently He Shall Lead Them: Robert Parris Moses and Civil Rights in Mississippi*. New York: New York University Press, 1994.

Chamberlain, Daphne Rochelle. "'And a Child Shall Lead the Way': Children's Participation in the Jackson, Mississippi, Black Freedom Struggle, 1946–1970." PhD diss., University of Mississippi, 2009.

Cobb, Charles E., Jr. *This Nonviolent Stuff'll Get You Killed: How Guns Made the Civil Rights Movement Possible*. Durham: Duke University Press, 2015.

Dent, Tom. *Southern Journey: A Return to the Civil Rights Movement*. New York: William Morrow and Company, 1997.

Dittmer, John. *Local People: The Struggle for Civil Rights in Mississippi*. Urbana: University of Illinois Press, 1994.

Evers, Medgar. "Why I Live in Mississippi." *Ebony*, November 1958.

Evers, Myrlie, with William Peters. *For Us, the Living*. Garden City: Doubleday & Company, 1967.

Evers-Williams, Myrlie, and Manning Marable, eds. *The Autobiography of Medgar Evers: A Hero's Life and Legacy Revealed Through His Writings, Letters, and Speeches*. New York: Basic Civitas Books, 2005.

Forman, James. *The Making of Black Revolutionaries*. Seattle and London: University of Washington Press, 1997.

Hale, Jon N. *The Freedom Schools: Student Activists in the Mississippi Civil Rights Movement.* New York: Columbia University Press, 2016.

_____. "'The Student as a Force for Social Change': The Mississippi Freedom Schools and Student Engagement." *Journal of African American History* 96, no. 3 (Summer 2011): 325–347.

Hamer, Fannie Lou. *To Praise Our Bridges.* Jackson: KIPCO, 1967.

Hampton, Henry, and Steve Fayer. *Voices of Freedom: An Oral History of the Civil Rights Movement from the 1950s through the 1980s.* New York: Bantam Books, 1990.

Hayden, Tom. *Revolution in Mississippi.* New York: Students for a Democratic Society, 1962.

Holland, Endesha Ida Mae. *From the Mississippi Delta: A Memoir.* Chicago: Lawrence Hill Books, 1997.

Hollis, Geraldine Edwards. *Back to Mississippi.* Bloomington: Xlibris, 2011.

Holsaert, Faith S. et al. *Hands on the Freedom Plow: Personal Accounts by Women in SNCC.* Urbana, Chicago, and Springfield: University of Illinois Press, 2010.

Holt, Len. *The Summer That Didn't End: The Story of the Mississippi Civil Rights Project of 1964.* New York: Da Capo Press, 1992.

Howe, Florence. "Mississippi's Freedom Schools: The Politics of Education." *Harvard Educational Review* 35, no. 2 (July 1965): 144–160.

Huie, William Bradford. "The Shocking Story of Approved Killing in Mississippi." *Look,* January 1956.

Larsson, Clotye Murdock. "Land of the Till Murder Revisited." *Ebony,* March 1986.

Lee, Chana Kai. *For Freedom's Sake: The Life of Fannie Lou Hamer.* Urbana: University of Illinois Press, 2000.

Martínez, Elizabeth, ed. *Letters from Mississippi: Reports from Civil Rights Volunteers & Poetry of the 1964 Freedom Summer.* Brookline: Zephyr Press, 2014.

McAdam, Doug. *Freedom Summer.* New York: Oxford University Press, 1988.

Mendelsohn, Jack. *The Martyrs: Sixteen Who Gave Their Lives for Racial Justice.* New York: Harper & Row Publishers, 1966.

Metress, Christopher, ed. *The Lynching of Emmett Till: A Documentary Narrative.* Charlottesville: University of Virginia Press, 2002.

Mills, Kay. *This Little Light of Mine: The Life of Fannie Lou Hamer.* New York: Plume, 1993.

Moody, Anne. *Coming of Age in Mississippi.* New York: Laurel, 1968.

Moses, Bob. "Mississippi: 1961–1962." *Liberation,* January 1970.

Moses, Robert P., and Charles E. Cobb Jr. *Radical Equations: Civil Rights from Mississippi to the Algebra Project.* Boston: Beacon Press, 2001.

O'Brien, M. J. *We Shall Not Be Moved: The Jackson Woolworth's Sit-In and the Movement It Inspired.* Jackson: University Press of Mississippi, 2013.

O'Dell, J. H. "Life in Mississippi: An Interview with Fannie Lou Hamer." In *Freedomways Reader: Prophets in Their Own Country*, edited by Esther Cooper Jackson, 97–99. Boulder: Westview Press, 2000.

Olson, Lynne. *Freedom's Daughters: The Unsung Heroines of the Civil Rights Movement from 1830 to 1970.* New York: Scribner, 2001.

Payne, Charles M. *I've Got the Light of Freedom: The Organizing Tradition and the Mississippi Freedom Struggle.* Berkeley: University of California Press, 1995.

Powdermaker, Hortense. *After Freedom: A Cultural Study in the Deep South.* New York: Russell & Russell, 1939.

"The Revolution." *Time*, June 7, 1963.

Romano, Tom. "The Power of Voice." *Educational Leadership*, October 2004.

Salter, John. *Jackson, Mississippi: An American Chronicle of Struggle and Schism.* Lincoln: University of Nebraska Press, 1979.

Sinsheimer, Joe. "Never Turn Back: An Interview with Sam Block." *Southern Exposure*, Summer 1987.

Smith, Jerome. "The Jump-off Point." In *My Soul Looks Back in Wonder: Voices of the Civil Rights Experience*, edited by Juan Williams, 60–64. New York: AARP, Sterling, 2004.

Travis, Brenda, and John Obee. *Mississippi's Exiled Daughter: How My Civil Rights Baptism Under Fire Shaped My Life.* Montgomery: NewSouth Books, 2018.

Tyson, Timothy B. *The Blood of Emmett Till.* New York: Simon & Schuster, 2017.

Umoja, Akinyele K. *We Will Shoot Back: Armed Resistance in the Mississippi Freedom Movement.* New York and London: New York University Press, 2013.

Wagner, Terry. "America's Civil Rights Revolution: Three Documentaries about Emmett Till's Murder in Mississippi." *Historical Journal of Film, Radio and Television* 30, no. 2 (June 2010): 187–201.

Warren, Robert Penn. "Two for SNCC." *Commentary*, April 1965.

Williams, Juan. *Eyes on the Prize: America's Civil Rights Years, 1954–1965.* New York: Penguin Books, 1987.

_____. *My Soul Looks Back in Wonder: Voices of the Civil Rights Experience.* New York: Sterling, 2004.

Williams, Michael Vinson. *Medgar Evers: Mississippi Martyr.* Fayetteville: The University of Arkansas Press, 2011.

Wright, Simeon. *Simeon's Story: An Eyewitness Account of the Kidnapping of Emmett Till.* Chicago: Chicago Review Press, 2011.

Zellner, Bob, with Constance Curry. *The Wrong Side of Murder Creek: A White Southerner in the Freedom Movement.* Montgomery: NewSouth Books, 2008.

WEBSITES AND VIDEOS

The internet contains an abundance of resources for studying the civil rights movement and specifically the freedom struggle in Mississippi. I used many of those resources to write this book. I encourage you to go to the sites listed and described below. Some even feature the voices of people who were part of the story told in these pages. For easy access, simply type the page name featured in the head of each entry in your favorite search engine. Each site can also be accessed directly by typing in the included URLs.

CIVIL RIGHTS MOVEMENT ARCHIVE: crmvet.org

This online archive is sponsored by people who actually served in the civil rights movement. These organizers want to share their own telling of the movement's history, explaining, "We ain't neutral." They do us all a service with the rich array of primary sources and photos contained in the archive. The website covers the entire movement in the South, including Mississippi.

DIGITAL SNCC GATEWAY: snccdigital.org/category/people

To learn about the story of SNCC, go to this website and encounter many of the people we have met in *In the Name of Emmett Till.* This website—full of rich history and powerful ideas—was made by people who love SNCC and have a desire to keep the legacy of the organization alive. SNCC and the people who shaped it come through in a vivid way via video, oral history, documents, photos, and sometimes just good explanation.

"An Evening with the Tougaloo Nine": youtube.com/
watch?v=0f_mG0hFvU4
In this wonderful forum, you can hear members of the Tougaloo Nine
share their inside version of the library sit-in narrative. The symposium
took place on October 6, 2015, and was sponsored by the Fannie Lou
Hamer Institute.

Famous Trials by Douglas O. Linder: famous-trials.com
Use this website to find documents from famous trials that took place
throughout history and all over the globe. Relevant to us, scroll down
and find items from the trial of Emmett Till's murderers, including pieces
of the trial transcript, a later FBI report, and the *Look* magazine article
with the killer's confession. If you continue your search, you will find
items from other trials that concern issues of race, including the trial of
George Zimmerman, the man who killed Trayvon Martin.

The Freedom Summer Text & Photo Archive, Miami University
Libraries, Digital Collections: digital.lib.miamioh.edu/digital/
collection/fstxt
This archive sponsored by Miami University in Oxford, Ohio, contains
a large collection of primary documents related to Freedom Summer.

Joseph A. Sinsheimer Papers, 1962–1987: library.duke.edu/
rubenstein/findingaids/sinsheimerjoseph/#aspace_ref623_tvi
On this site you will find interviews with many people involved in the
civil rights movement, including some of the most important people
who participated in the Mississippi Freedom Struggle. Scroll down to
the big green "online access" box and click on "only view items with
online access" to discover interviews with people you met in this book,
including Sam Block, Endesha Ida Mae Holland, June Johnson, Dr.
Joyce Ladner, Silas McGhee, and Robert Moses. It is amazing to hear
the actual voices of these activists. You can even listen to an interview
with Dr. Leslie-Burl McLemore, who wrote the foreword to *In the Name
of Emmett Till*.

LIBRARY OF CONGRESS, CIVIL RIGHTS HISTORY PROJECT: loc.gov/
collections/civil-rights-history-project
This collection includes video oral histories of many people who were
active in the civil rights movement. Three oral histories have particular
relevance to this book: Simeon Wright, Dorie Ann Ladner and Joyce
Ladner, and Amos C. Brown.

MISSISSIPPI SOVEREIGNTY COMMISSION ONLINE: mdah.ms.gov/arrec/
digital_archives/sovcom
The Mississippi Sovereignty Commission came into existence in 1956.
One of its main tasks was to monitor the activities of people in the
Mississippi civil rights movement. The Commission ceased functioning
in 1977. Today all records from the Commission are available online,
providing a warehouse of documents for historians and anyone else
interested in the civil rights movement. Go to the site and put in the
name of anyone mentioned in *In the Name of Emmett Till* and you are
likely to gain access to materials related to that person, including newspaper articles, arrest records, reports from Commission spies, photos,
and much more.

PACIFICA RADIO ARCHIVES: soundcloud.com/pacificaradioarchives
The Pacifica Radio Archives contain an interview with Joseph Jackson of
the Tougaloo Nine. Place "Joseph Jackson Jr. Tougaloo 9" in the search
function to find the conversation. Recordings within the archive come
from radio stations that were part of the Pacifica Radio network. This
network of early listener-sponsored stations started in 1949.

SOUTHERN JOURNEY ORAL HISTORY COLLECTION, TOM DENT: digitalli-
brary.tulane.edu/islandora/object/tulane%3Adent
Between 1991 and 1994 writer Tom Dent traveled throughout the South
collecting oral histories from people involved in the civil rights movement. He used those interviews to write his book, *Southern Journey: A
Return to the Civil Rights Movement*. As a part of his travels he stopped
in Mississippi, interviewing people from Canton, including Ms. Annie
Devine and Jewel Williams. Scroll down the page to find "Mississippi-
Canton: Annie Devine and Jewel Williams Interviewees" and click on
the microphone to hear the multi-part interview.

SPEAK NOW: MEMORIES OF THE CIVIL RIGHTS ERA IN THE MISSISSIPPI ARCHIVES: mdah.ms.gov/arrec/digital_archives/speaknow
The Speak Now website contains an audio interview with Amos Brown along with a transcript. The site contains the interviews of others active in the civil rights movement as well. Click the "List Interviews" link near the bottom of the page to display all available interviews and then click "AU 982 - Rev. (Dr.) Amos Brown."

TELLING THEIR STORIES: VETERANS OF THE CIVIL RIGHTS STRUGGLE IN MCCOMB, MISSISSIPPI: tellingstories.org/mccomb
This site contains a collection of interviews from various people involved in the McComb, Mississippi, freedom struggle of the sixties. The interviews were done by high school students from McComb and San Francisco. Many of the interviews focus specifically on the Burglund High School walkouts. The students interviewed Brenda Travis, Curtis Muhammad, Joe Lewis, and others. Brenda Travis, in particular, tells her story in a dramatic manner.

DIGITAL COLLECTIONS, THE UNIVERSITY OF SOUTHERN MISSISSIPPI: digilib.usm.edu/crmda.php
This archive includes interviews with many people involved in the civil rights movement. Put the names of activists into the search bar to find resources, including an audio interview with John Frazier and a remarkable set of Freedom Summer photos from Herbert Randall.

WISCONSIN HISTORICAL SOCIETY, 1964 FREEDOM SUMMER PROJECT: content.wisconsinhistory.org/cdm/landingpage/collection/p15932coll2
Find out much more about Freedom Summer with this amazing collection that includes both documents and photographs. The photos make Freedom Summer come to life.

Notes

. . . .

CHAPTER 1: EMMETT TILL, THE BEGINNING

Robert Hodges's account of finding Till's body is drawn from the 1955 trial transcript of *State of Mississippi v. J. W. Milam and Roy Bryant* in the circuit court of Tallahatchie County, as are the later statements of Mose Wright and Willie Reed. The sheriff's and police statements about the condition of the body are from Cloyte Murdock Larsson, "Land of the Till Murder Revisited," *Ebony* (March, 1986), and Devery S. Anderson, *Emmett Till: The Murder that Shocked the World and Propelled the Civil Rights Movement* (University Press of Mississippi, 2015), 46. Anderson also references Mose Wright. Mamie Till-Mobley's comments are as told to the *Chicago Defender* in 1955 and 1956 and reprinted in Christopher Metress, ed., *The Lynching of Emmett Till: A Documentary Narrative* (University of Virginia Press, 2002), 30, 228.

Curtis Jones's remembrance of his late cousin is from a 1985 interview conducted by Blackside, Inc., for *Eyes on the Prize: America's Civil Rights Years (1954–1965),* Washington Film and Media Archive, Henry Hampton Collection (https://library.wustl.edu/spec/eyesontheprize). The events of the night before Till was kidnapped, then the murder, then the trial are drawn from the trial transcript and from Timothy B. Tyson, *The Blood of Emmett Till* (Simon & Schuster, 2017), 6; Simeon Wright, *Simeon's Story: An Eyewitness Account of the Kidnapping of Emmett Till* (Chicago Review Press, 2011), 50–51; and Simeon Booker, *Shocking the Conscience: A Reporter's Account of the Civil Rights Movement* (University Press of Mississippi, 2013), 62. That today more are suspected of being involved is from Terry Wagner, "America's Civil Rights Revolution: Three Documentaries About Emmett Till's Murder In Mississippi," *Historical Journal of Film, Radio and Television* 30, 2 (June 2010): 187–201.

The comments of the murderers after they were acquitted were told to William Bradford Huie, "The Shocking Story of Approved Killing in Mississippi," *Look* magazine (January 1956): 46–50. Mamie Till-Mobley's later comments were to Juan Williams, *Eyes on the Prize: America's Civil Rights Years, 1954–1965* (Penguin Books, 1987), 57. Joyce Ladner's assessment of Till's significance is in Faith Holsaert, et al., *Hands on the Freedom Plow: Personal Accounts by Women in SNCC.* (University of Illinois Press, 2010), 219.

ELDERS I—MEDGAR EVERS JOINS THE FIGHT FOR FREEDOM

Medgar Evers's return to Mississippi after serving World War II is described in Michael Vinson Williams, *Medgar Evers: Mississippi Martyr* (University of Arkansas Press, 2011), 33–4.

Discussions of Evers's early life comes from Medgar Evers (as told to Francis H. Mitchell), "Why I Live in Mississippi," *Ebony*, November 1958, in Myrlie Evers-Williams and Manning Marable, eds., *The Autobiography of Medgar Evers: A Hero's Life and Legacy Revealed Through his Writings, Letters, and Speeches* (Basic Civitas Books, 2005), 112, 33–4, 41

Myrlie Evers's remembrances of her husband's life as an activist comes from an interview contained in Henry Hampton and Steve Fayer, *Voices of Freedom: An Oral History of the Civil Rights Movement from the 1950s through the 1980s* (Bantam Books, 1990), 6, and Myrlie Evers with William Peters, *For Us, the Living* (Doubleday & Company, 1967), 172.

Shirley Harrington-Watson's thoughts on Evers come from her talk: "Remembering the 1963 Jackson Children's March" from the 30th Annual Fannie Lou Hamer Memorial Symposium: The Children's Crusade, 1963–2013, Jackson State University, Jackson, Mississippi, October 3, 2013.

CHAPTER 2: THE TOUGALOO NINE AND THE LADNER SISTERS

The Ladners describe their early life as well as their time at Jackson State College in interviews: Faith Holsaert, et al., 217, 218 (Joyce Ladner); Joyce Ladner, May 23, 1986, with Joseph A. Sinsheimer, Guide to the Joseph A. Sinsheimer Papers,1962–1987, Duke University Libraries, https://library.duke.edu/rubenstein/findingaids/sinsheimerjoseph/; both Ladners with Joseph Mosnier, Library of Congress, September 20, 2011.

Members of the Tougaloo Nine share their perspective on the library sit-in in Eric Barrow, "*Unsung Heroes of Civil Rights*" New York Daily News, February 15, 2016; see also Mary Kathryn Carpenter, "Activist remembers Tougaloo nine protest," *Natchez Democrat,* July 4, 2014; look up "Evening with the Tougaloo Nine" on YouTube.com to see a discussion at the 28th Annual FLH Symposium, October 6, 2015; see also John Dittmer, *Local People: The Struggle for Civil Rights in Mississippi* (University of Illinois Press, 1994), 87; see Joseph Jackson interview with Gabriel San Roman, May 31, 2015, at fromthevaultradio.org; Edmund Noell, "Nine Jailed in 'Study-In,'" Jackson *Clarion-Ledger*, March 28, 1961; and Mike O'Brien, "Civil Rights Era Revisited: The Tougaloo Nine/ The Woolworth Sit-In/Civil Rights" at www.blogtalkradio.com/gumboforthesoul/2014/10/23/civil-rights-era-revisited-the-tougaloo-9-the-woolworth-sit-in-civil-rights.

Some description of the Jackson State College student march comes from "Police Halt March by Negro Students in Mississippi," *New York Times,* March 29, 1961.

The trial of the Tougaloo Nine and events surrounding the trial are reported in "Monthly Report: 'Desegregation Activities' April 21, 1961" in Evers-Williams and Marable, eds., 228; "Arguments end in Mixing Case," *United Press International,* March 13, 1962; and Geraldine Edwards Hollis, *Back to Mississippi* (Xlibris, 2011), 129.

Views about the Nine from Medgar and Myrlie Evers can be found in "Medgar Evers to Roy Wilkins, March 29, 1961" in Evers-Williams and Marable, 223–4; and Evers with Peters, 235.

CHAPTER 3: THE "CHILDREN" OF MEDGAR EVERS

Amos Brown's talk about his life and civil rights activities comes from the following sources: interview with David P. Cline, Library of Congress, March 2, 2013; interview with LeAnna Welch, Mississippi Department of Archives and History, May 27, 2011; and Nancy Watzman, "In Search of Not-So-Lost Time: What Transparency Can Tell Us about History, Race Relations and Ferguson," in the sunlightfoundation.com blog, December. 1, 2014; and W. C. Shoemaker, "Negroes Declare Aimed to Agitate," *Jackson Daily News,* March 12, 1962.

The sheriff's comments about the George Lee murder are in Jack Mendelsohn, *The Martyrs: Sixteen Who Gave their Lives for Racial Justice* (Harper & Row, Publishers, 1966), 6.

Ideas guiding San Francisco's Third Baptist Church where Amos Brown pastors today come from "Welcome to Third Baptist, A Servant Church for All People" at thirdbaptist.org/who-we-are/.

Johnny Frazier's recollections of his life, civil rights activities, and his feelings about Medgar Evers can be found in his interview with Nishani Frazier, University of Southern Mississippi, Digital Collections, March 21, 2004; see also reports of his civil rights activities taken from Zack J. Van Landingham, March 11, 1960, Mississippi Sovereignty Commission Online at www.mdah.ms.gov, and Tom Scarbrough, April 16, 1961, at the same source. See also Commission records at http://www.mdah.ms.gov/arrec/digital_archives/sovcom/.

ELDERS II—THE EDUCATION OF BOB MOSES

Bob Moses shares recollections of his early life and his entry into the movement in Robert P. Moses and Charles E. Cobb, Jr., *Radical Equations: Civil Rights from Mississippi to the Algebra Project* (Beacon Press, 2001), 3. See also: Robert Moses interview, National Visionary Leadership Project, www.visionaryproject. org/mosesrobert/; Eric Burner, *And Gently He Shall Lead Them: Robert Parris Moses and Civil Rights in Mississippi* (New York University Press, 1994), 11; and Robert Penn Warren, "Two for SNCC," *Commentary,* April 1965, 39. Also in Burner, a Hamilton College student comments about the college atmosphere, 11.

CHAPTER 4: BRENDA TRAVIS AND THE BURGLUND WALKOUT

Brenda Travis describes her early life and later civil rights activities in an interview with McComb High School students, Telling Their Stories: Oral History Archives Project, May 6 and 7, 2010, at www.tellingstories.org/mccomb/ fullmovies/travis_brenda/index.html. See also the interview with Wazir Peacock, Jean Wiley and Bruce Hartford at the Veterans of the Civil Rights Movement Website, February, 2007,www.crmvet.org/nars/travisb.htm. The comment about "The greatest act of bravery I've ever seen" is from a story by Steve Marion of the

Standard Banner at http://www.cn.edu/news?view=225. See also Travis's interview with Owen Brooks at www.crmvet.org/audio/msoh/2007_travis_brenda.mp3 (or search in a browser window for "Brenda Travis CRMVET") and Lynne Olson, *Freedom's Daughters: The Unsung Heroes of the Civil Rights Movement from 1830 to 1970* (Scribner, 2001), 206.

Hollis Watkins lays out his movement life in his interviews with John Rachal, University of Southern Mississippi's Center for Oral History and Cultural Heritage, October 23 and 30, 1995, http://digilib.usm.edu/cdm/compoundobject/collection/coh/id/15282/rec/8, and with Blackside, Inc., November 9, 1985, for *Eyes on the Prize: America's Civil Rights Years (1954–1965)*, Washington Film and Media Archive, Henry Hampton Collection at digital.wwustl.edu/e/eop/eopweb/wat0015.0448.108holliswatkins.html.

The description of McComb's SNCC headquarters as well as a discussion of Hollis Watkins and Curtis Hayes's activism can be found in James Forman, *The Making of Black Revolutionaries* (University of Washington Press, 1997), 225.

Bob Moses shared his comments about Brenda Travis in "Mississippi: 1961–1962," *Liberation*, January 1970, 10–11.

Joe Lewis's take on the Burglund High School Walkout and the student march into town can be found in his interview with McComb High School students, Telling Their Stories: Oral History Archives Project, March 26, 2011.

The student march into McComb and the subsequent rally on the courthouse steps are described by Bob Zellner, *The Wrong Side of Murder Creek: A White Southerner in the Freedom Movement* (NewSouth Books, 2008), 157.

Tom Hayden shares a detail about the student rally on the McComb courthouse steps in *Revolution in Mississippi: Special Report* (New York: Students for a Democratic Society, January, 1962), 18. From Civil Rights Digital Library, digilib.usm.edu/cdm/compoundobject/collection/manu/id/3563/rec/1.

Brenda Travis's reflections on her civil rights activities can be found in Natalie A. Collier, "Better Late Than Never," *Jackson Free Press*, June 28, 2006.

CHAPTER 5: FREEDOM RIDERS AND TWO KIDS FROM JACKSON

Descriptions of Freedom Riders coming into McComb can be found in Juan Williams, *My Soul Looks Back in Wonder: Voices of the Civil Rights Experience*. (Sterling Publishing Co., Inc., 2004), 61; and Claude Sitton, "5 Negroes Beaten by Mississippi Mob," *New York Times*, November 30, 1961.

The wording for the sign on buses that the Interstate Commerce Commission required and comments from a Klansman and a Freedom Rider can be found in Raymond Arsenault, *Freedom Riders: 1961 and the Struggle for Racial Justice*. (Oxford University Press, 2006), 429, 145; see also Taylor Branch, *Parting the Waters: America in the King Years, 1954–63*. (Simon and Schuster, 1988), 424.

Luvaughn Brown talks about growing up in Jackson and his movement life in Eric Barrow, "*Unsung Heroes of Civil Rights*" *New York Daily News*, February 15, 2016.

Luvaughn Brown and Jimmie Travis's arrest report is available on L. D. Holliday,

"Offense Report," from Mississippi Sovereignty Commission Online, www.mdah. ms.gov/arrec/digital_archives/sovcom.

Comments on the Brown/Travis arrest come from W. C. Shoemaker, "2 Arrested in Counter Mix Move," *Jackson Clarion-Ledger*, July 10, 1961.

Brown's activities during the trial of Diane Nash are presented in "2 from Jackson Movement Jailed," *Student Voice*, June 2, 1962, content.wisconsinhistory. org/cdm/ref/collection/p15932coll2/id/50115.

Hezekiah Watkins shares the story of his early days and his life in the movement in Drew Jansen, "Freedom Riders Tell their Stories as Part of Discussion Panel," *Daily Mississippian Online*, thedmarchives.com/freedom-riders-tell-their-stories-as-part-of-discussion-panel/; see also Matthew Caston, "Four Views from Jackson: Reflections on the Anticipated Ride to Freedom—May, 1961," *Jackson Advocate*, May 25, 2011; and Hezekiah Watkins interview with Rick Smith, August 20, 2015, in The Rick Smith Show Podcast, www.podbean.com/media/share/pb-cej74–581b42.

CHAPTER 6: THE NORTH JACKSON YOUTH COUNCIL

Claudette Colvin's words come from Elissa Blattman, "The Girl Who Acted Before Rosa Parks," on the website of the National Women's History Museum, www.womenshistory.org/articles/girl-who-acted-rosa-parks. Colia Liddell Lafayette Clark relates her growing up in a July 24, 2008, interview with Harold Hudson Channer; search Youtube.com for her name and his.

Descriptions of State Fair protests come from Dittmer, 117, and M. J. O'Brien, *We Shall Not Be Moved: The Jackson Woolworth's Sit-In and the Movement It Inspired.* (University Press of Mississippi, 2013), 57.

The confrontation between Medgar Evers and Mayor Thompson is discussed in John Salter, *Jackson, Mississippi: An American Chronicle of Struggle and Schism.* (University of Nebraska Press, 1979), 110, 120, 130 and O'Brien, 107, 109, 111.

Accounts of what took place during the Woolworth's sit-in come from a variety of sources including Dittmer, 161, 162; O'Brien, 120, 125, 127, 131–2, 135, 144, 146, 148, 150; Anne Moody, *Coming of Age in Mississippi* (Laurel, 1968), 266, 268, and "The Revolution," *Time* magazine, June 7, 1963, 17.

CHAPTER 7: THE CHILDREN OF JACKSON MARCH

The sources conveying the narrative of the Lanier High walkout include "Jackson Police Jail 600 Negro Children," *New York Times*, June 1, 1963, 1; "White Minister Held in Jackson," *New York Times*, May 31, 1963, 26; Hezekiah Watkins interview with Don Williams, Jackson Civil Rights Sites Project, Margaret Walker Alexander Research Center, September 17, 1998, www.mshistorynow.mdah.ms.gov/articles/60/index.php?s=extra&id=260; and Daphne Rochelle Chamberlain, "'And a Child Shall Lead the Way': Children's Participation in the Jackson, Mississippi, Black Freedom Struggle, 1946–1970" (PhD diss., University of Mississippi, 2009), 151.

Descriptions of the Children's March, the subsequent evening rally, and later protests can be found in O'Brien, 163, 164, 165, 168, 170; "Negro Trains Corps for Jackson Sit-Ins," *New York Times,* May 31, 1963, 1; Chamberlain, 147; Salter, 149, 152, 153, 154, 155; "The Battle of Jackson," *Newsweek,* June 10, 1963, 29, and "Jackson Police Jail 600 Negro Children," *New York Times,* June 1, 1963, 1.

CHAPTER 8: A TRAGEDY AND A PEOPLE'S REACTION

President Kennedy's civil rights address can be found in Robert H. Mayer ed., *The Civil Rights Act of 1964.* (Farmington Hills, Mich.: Greenhaven Press, 2004), 21–2.

Myrlie Evers shares her thoughts the evening of Medgar Evers's assassination in Evers with Peters, 300, 301. Activists' reaction to the assassination can be found in Moody, 276, and Salter, 188.

The protests and rally that occur the day after the assassination as well as actions after that day are discussed in Salter, 188, 189, 192, 193, 194, 195; "N.A.A.C.P. Leader Slain in Jackson; Protests Mount," *New York Times,* June 13, 1963, 1; O'Brien, 208; and "Jackson Negroes Clubbed as Police Quell Marchers," *New York Times,* June 14, 1963, 1.

The narrative of Medgar Evers's funeral, the community commemorative march, and aftermath are constructed from: O'Brien, 209, 210, 214–6, 218, 228; Salter, 211; Moody, 281; "27 are Arrested in Jackson Riots after Evers Rite," *New York Times,* June 16, 1963, 1; Michael Vinson Williams, 291; and "Jackson Mayor Agrees to Meet Some Demands in Negro Drive," *New York Times,* June 19, 1963, 32.

ELDERS III—THE SAGA OF FANNIE LOU HAMER

The story of Fannie Lou Hamer's early life and her later activism come from interviews, J. H. O'Dell, "Life in Mississippi: An Interview with Fannie Lou Hamer," No. 2, 1965, in Esther Cooper Jackson, ed., *Freedomways Reader: Prophets in Their Own Country* (Westview Press, 2000), 98; and Fannie Lou Hamer, interview with Neil McMillen, University of Southern Mississippi's Center for Oral History and Cultural Heritage, April 14, 1972, http://digilib.usm.edu/cdm/ref/collection/coh/id/15272; contemporary reporting, Phyl Garland, "Builders of a New South: Negro Heroines of Dixie Play Major Role in Challenging Racist Traditions," *Ebony,* August 1966, 28; and secondary sources: Kay Mills, *This Little Light of Mine: The Life of Fannie Lou Hamer* (Plume, 1993), 24, 36, 37, 38, 39, and Chana Kai Lee, *For Freedom's Sake: The Life of Fannie Lou Hamer* (University of Illinois Press, 2000), 37.

The description of sharecropping comes from Fannie Lou Hamer, interview with Neil McMillen, University of Southern Mississippi's Center for Oral History and Cultural Heritage, April 14, 1972, http://digilib.usm.edu/cdm/ref/collection/coh/id/15272, and Garland, 28. The presentation of white attitudes is part of this study done in the thirties: Hortense Powdermaker, *After Freedom: A Cultural Study in the Deep South.* (New York: Russell & Russell, 1939), 88, 329, 382.

Chapter 9: Greenwood Part 1—
Sam Block Shakes Things Up

Much of the direct account of Sam Block and the Greenwood movement comes from an interview shared in these two sources: Joe Sinsheimer, "Never Turn Back: An Interview with Sam Block," *Southern Exposure,* Summer 1987, 40, 41, 43, 44 and the Block interview in the Sinsheimer Papers, November 19, 1998, as well as reports by Block and Jimmy Travis included in Forman, 283, 294–5. Adding to that telling are Dittmer, 132, 149, and Charles Payne, *I've Got the Light of Freedom: The Organizing Tradition and the Mississippi Freedom Struggle* (University of California Press, 1995), 161, 163.

Chapter 10: Greenwood Part II—The Children

Much of the telling of June Johnson's life, including her life as a SNCC activist, comes from her own account in a November 29, 1998, interview in the Sinsheimer Papers, and David Welsh, "Valley of Fear," *Ramparts,* Special Issue, 1964, 61, and Olson, 206. In addition to Johnson's telling of the arrest and beatings in Winona, a secondary account with other voices comes from Dittmer, 170, 171–2.

Septima Clark's identification as "mother of the movement" is noted in Jackie Johnson, etv, "Septima Clark: SC Hall of Fame," https://www.scetv.org/stories/2020/septima-clark-sc-hall-fame.

Endesha Ida Mae Holland's story from early life to activism to later life is told in a March 14, 1987, interview in the Sinsheimer Papers; in Endesha Ida Mae Holland, *From the Mississippi Delta: A Memoir* (Lawrence Hill Books, 1997), 87, 201, 204, 208, 210, 217, 227, 253, 313; and "Endesha Ida Mae Holland" Encyclopedia.com. A comment from Holland and another from Mayor Charles Sampson comes from Dittmer, 151, 154.

A firsthand description of a Greenwood march is shared in Claude Sitton, "Police Loose a Dog on Negroes' Group; Minister is Bitten," *New York Times,* March 29, 1963.

Silas McGhee presents his life as an activist, integrating movie theaters and facing attacks from racist Whites in a December 1, 1998, interview in the Sinsheimer Papers and in Eric Moskowitz, "They heard the call of freedom, a summons that still haunts," *Boston Globe,* August 31, 2014. The story of the July 16 assault on McGhee is in "FBI Makes First Arrests Under Civil Rights Act," *The Blade,* July 24, 1964. Linda Whetmore Halpern shares her experience of taking McGhee to the hospital in "The Shooting of Silas McGhee," Veterans of the Civil Rights Movement (The Celebration of the 50th Anniversary of the Student-Led Sit-ins of 1960, the Rise of Youth-Led Activism, and the Founding of SNCC, Main library, San Francisco), March 27, 2010, www.crmvet.org/nars/stor/s_linda.htm.

Chapter 11: George Raymond in Canton

George Raymond and the Canton movement are discussed in: Jewel Williams, interview with Tom Dent, Southern Journey Oral History Collection, Tulane University Digital Library, September 18, 1991, https://digitallibrary.tulane.

edu/islandora/object/tulane%3A54092h; Ed Hollander, "Report on Canton Jan. 25–30 incl," January 31, 1964, archived in Mississippi Sovereignty Commission Online, SCR ID # 2-24-2-20-1-1-1, http://www.mdah.ms.gov/arrec/digital_archives/sovcom/result.php?image=images/png/cd01/004900.png&other stuff=2|24|2|20|1|1|1|4780|; and "Statement Made by George Raymond, Canton Project Leader on Freedom Day, February 28, 1964, At Pleasant Green Church," archived in Wisconsin Historical Society, Freedom Summer Collection, https://www.wisconsinhistory.org/Records/Image/IM125797).

The statement about Canton comes from Akinyele K. Umoja, *We Will Shoot Back: Armed Resistance in the Mississippi Freedom Movement* (New York: New York University Press, 2013), 116.

C.O. Chinn's readiness to use guns and his overall role in the Canton movement are presented in "C.O. Chinn" Digital SNCC Gateway, https://snccdigital.org/people/c-o-chinn/; Charles E. Cobb, *This Nonviolent Stuff'll Get You Killed: How Guns Made the Civil Rights Movement Possible* (Duke University Press, 2015), 190; and Matt ("Flukey") Suarez, interview with Harriet Tanzman, Veterans of the Civil Rights Movement, March 26 and 30, 2000, http://www.crmvet.org/nars/suarez.htm.

Annie Devine's role as an organizer in Canton, before and during the 1964 Canton movement can be found in Tom Dent's interview with Jewel Williams; Dittmer, 190; and Tom Dent, *Southern Journey: A Return to the Civil Rights Movement.* (William Morrow and Company, Inc., 1977), 347.

Anne Moody's organizing of young people in Canton is presented in Moody, 293, 326; and Dittmer, 189.

Accounts of the stores boycott, voter registration drive, and Freedom Days are taken from Phil Mullen, "Canton Merchants Will Tell Facts on Boycott, *Clarion-Ledger,* January 16, 1964, and Claude Sitton, "Negro Queue in Mississippi is Symbol of Frustration in Voter Registration Drive," *New York Times,* March 2, 1964, 20; and clippings of news articles—Dudley Lehew, "Few Negroes out in Canton Drive," *Jackson Clarion Ledger,* March 1, 1964; "'Too Slow' Cries Leader; 'Less Cops, More Clerks," *Mississippi Free Press,* March 7, 1964—that are archived in the Wisconsin Historical Society Freedom Summer Collection, which also contains these useful documents that touch on the store and school boycotts, voter registration, and Freedom Days: "Fact Sheet on a School Boycott and School Integration"; statement by Gus Noble of the White Citizen's Council in "White Community - fact sheet (1964)"; "Field Report, Canton, Mississippi," Memoranda, Clippings, March 13, 1964"; "Fact Sheet on Voter Registration and Freedom Days," CORE—-Canton Project history (1964)—Memoranda, 1965; T. W. Simer, "Memorandum on a Three Day Visit to Canton, Mississippi. March 1–4, and Huber Klemme, "A Report of a Visit to Canton Mississippi, February 26–29" (CORE—Ministers' Reports on Visits, Committee Projects of National Council of Churches and United Church of Christ). The Wisconsin Historical Commission Freedom Summer Collection can be browsed at www.wisconsinhistory.org/Records/Article/CS15293.

CHAPTER 12: FREEDOM SUMMER, FREEDOM SCHOOLS, A LEGACY OF ACTIVISM

The Freedom Schools' curriculum and philosophy are presented in Jon Hale, *The Freedom Schools: Student Activists in the Mississippi Civil Rights Movement* (Columbia University Press, 2016), 94. First-person teacher accounts are in: Elizabeth Martinez (ed.), *Letters from Mississippi: Reports from Civil Rights Volunteers & Poetry of the 1964 Freedom Summer* (Zephyr Press, 2014), 106, 108, 111, 114–5, 116; Florence Howe, "Mississippi's Freedom Schools: The Politics of Education, " *Harvard Educational Review*, 35 (2), July 1965, 145, 157; George W. Chilcoat and Jerry A. Ligon, "'We Will Teach What Democracy Really Means by Living Democratically Within Our Own Schools' Lessons from the Personal Experience of Teachers Who Taught in the Mississippi Freedom Schools," *Education and Culture*, 11, no. 3 (1995), 38; and William Sturkey, "'I Want to Become a Part of History': Freedom Summer, Freedom Schools, and the Freedom News," *Journal of African American History*, 95, no. 3–4 (2010): 359.

Freedom Schools student writing is shared in: *Freedom School Poetry* (SNCC, 1965, www.crmvet.org/poetry/64_fskool_poems-r.pdf), 18, 20, 29, archived in the Freedom Summer Text & Photo Archive, Miami University Libraries, Digital Collections; Martinez, 111; and Len Holt, *The Summer that Didn't End: The Story of the Mississippi Civil Rights Project of 1964* (Da Capo Press, 1965), 110; and also in the newspapers *Student Voice of Truelight*, July 20, 1964, 2, 5, 6, *Freedom Press* (archived in Civil Rights Digital Library, http://crdl.usg.edu), and William Sturkey, *Freedom News*, July 23, 1964, 3 (archived in Wisconsin Historical Society, Freedom Summer Digital Collection, https://content.wisconsinhistory.org/digital/collection/p15932coll2).

First-person student accounts of activism during Freedom Summer and after can be found in Sandra E. Adickes, *Legacy of a Freedom School* (Palgraves Macmillan, 2005), 62, 90. 91; Jon Hale, *The Freedom Schools: Student Activists in the Mississippi Civil Rights Movement* (New York: Columbia University Press, 2016), 133, 160; and Jon Hale, "'The Student as a Force for Social Change': The Mississippi Freedom Schools and Student Engagement." *The Journal of African American History* 96, no. 3 (2011), 335, 336. The latter by Hale also discusses at 344 the legacy of Mississippi Freedom Schools as does "CDF Freedom Schools Program," Children's Defense Fund, https://www.childrensdefense.org/programs/cdf-freedom-schools/16.

Index

....